Your Guide To Financial Freedom:
How To Stop Living From Paycheck To Paycheck

How To Deal With Debt Collectors And Win Every Time How To Beat Them At Their Own Game: Your Number One Guide To Beating Debt Collectors

Credit Repair How To Repair Your Credit All By Yourself A Beginners Guide To Better Credit: Learn How To Repair Your Credit The Right Way

By

Ernie Braveboy

Get Your Free Copy of

How to be a Real Estate

Millionaire

To Get Your Free Copy, Open the Link

https://ebraveboy_3ee2.gr8.com/

TABLE OF CONTENTS

Your Guide To Financial Freedom: How To Stop Living From Paycheck To Paycheck   1

Introduction   3

Part 1: Understanding The Paycheck To Paycheck Phenomenon   7

Part 2: Stemming The Bleeding   16

Part 3: Moving Past The Beginner Level & Planting Your Financial Feet On Firm Ground   23

Part 4: Doing More To Be More: 44

Conclusion   53

How to Deal with Debt Collectors and Win Every Time How To Beat Them at Their Own Game   55

Introduction   57

Chapter 1: How Debt Collection Agencies Work   61

Chapter 2: What Debt Collection Agencies are NOT Allowed to Do   65

Chapter 3: What to Do When a Debt Collector Contacts You   72

Chapter 4: How to Beat a Debt Collection Agent in Court   103

Conclusion   116

Credit Repair: How to Repair Your Credit All by Yourself: A Beginners Guide to Better Credit   117

Introduction   119

Section 1: Understanding Credit & Credit Score   123

Chapter 1: Understanding Your Credit Score   124

Chapter 2: Understanding Credit Reports   127

Chapter 3: What Makes a Credit Score Excellent or Poor   131

Chapter 4: Why Repair Poor Credit   136

Section 2: Negative Items on the Credit Report   139

Chapter 5: Evaluating Negative Items That May Appear On Your Credit Report   140

Section 3: Overhauling Your Credit State   145

Chapter 6: Step 1 – Thoroughly Evaluate Each Credit Report   146

Chapter 7: Step 2 – Pinpoint the Credit Score Killers   149

Chapter 8: Step 3 – Clean Up the Credit Reports   152

Chapter 9: Step 4 – Evaluate Accounts in Collections & Continue Closely Monitoring Your Credit   157

Chapter 10: Step 5 – Start a Positive Credit History 160

Section 4: Tried & Tested Tips That Will Boost Your Credit Score Fast 163

Chapter 11: Quick Strategies You Can Implement To Give Your Credit a New Look in a Short Time 164

Section 5: What to Expect (and What Next) After Fixing Your Credit Score 169

Chapter 12: How Long It Takes To Overhaul Your Credit Score 170

Chapter 13: What To Do To Keep Your Credit Health Excellent 173

Bonus Section: Mortgage Application and Poor Credit Score 177

Bonus: A Mini-Guide on Mortgage Application for Those with Poor Credit 178

Conclusion 181

ERNIE BRAVEBOY

YOUR GUIDE TO FINANCIAL FREEDOM:

HOW TO STOP LIVING FROM PAYCHECK TO PAYCHECK

YOUR GUIDE TO FINANCIAL FREEDOM

ERNIE BRAVEBOY

INTRODUCTION

I want to thank you and congratulate you for buying the book, "Your Guide To Financial Freedom: How to Stop Living From Paycheck to Paycheck".

While money cannot buy happiness, having enough gives one peace of mind and because of the nature of money as a resource, opens up opportunities that ultimately lead to happiness.

Consider this; if you are wanderlust at heart, without enough money, you cannot fulfill this dream. The same happens to be the case with everything. If you do not have enough money, you cannot comfortably pay your bills, meet all your obligations, eat out, or even treat yourself (or your family) to something nice.

While "more money" is probably something all of us would love, even more, important than more money is the need to manage the money that you have right now. Without effective money management skills, you will live from paycheck to paycheck, always struggling to get ahead in life or have enough to do the things that matter the most to you.

This book is a money management guide that outlines, dissects, and then thoroughly discusses money management principles that when applied, will steer you away from debt and living from paycheck to paycheck, and onto the path to financial freedom.

Before we get started, it is important to note that financial freedom is a process, a process that requires discipline and a lot of patience. These two are the prerequisite and with them instilled, you can achieve financial independence irrespective of your current financial state, how much debt you have, and irrespective of your current income level.

Thanks again for buying this book. I hope you enjoy it!

ERNIE BRAVEBOY

© Copyright Ernie Braveboy 2018 - All rights reserved.

This document is geared towards providing exact and reliable information in regards to the topic and issue covered. The publication is sold with the idea that the publisher is not required to render accounting, officially permitted, or otherwise, qualified services. If advice is necessary, legal or professional, a practiced individual in the profession should be ordered.

- From a Declaration of Principles which was accepted and approved equally by a Committee of the American Bar Association and a Committee of Publishers and Associations.

In no way is it legal to reproduce, duplicate, or transmit any part of this document in either electronic means or in printed format. Recording of this publication is strictly prohibited and any storage of this document is not allowed unless with written permission from the publisher. All rights reserved.

The information provided herein is stated to be truthful and consistent, in that any liability, in terms of inattention or otherwise, by any usage or abuse of any policies, processes, or directions contained within is the solitary and utter responsibility of the recipient reader. Under no circumstances will any legal responsibility or blame be held against the publisher for any reparation, damages, or monetary loss due to the information herein, either directly or indirectly.

YOUR GUIDE TO FINANCIAL FREEDOM

Respective authors own all copyrights not held by the publisher.

The information herein is offered for informational purposes solely and is universal as so. The presentation of the information is without contract or any type of guarantee assurance.

The trademarks that are used are without any consent, and the publication of the trademark is without permission or backing by the trademark owner. All trademarks and brands within this book are for clarifying purposes only and are the owned by the owners themselves, not affiliated with this document.

Part 1: Understanding the Paycheck to Paycheck Phenomenon

The chapters that make up this part of the book are what we would call introductory chapters. Their aim is to illustrate the problem, i.e. the problem of living from paycheck to paycheck and trying to explain possible reasons why more than ¾ of the American populace is living from paycheck to paycheck. ☐

CHAPTER 1: PAY IN, PAY OUT, AN AMERICAN STORY

If someone developed a prime time, reality TV show of real-life examples of paycheck to paycheck living, one gets the feeling that it could run for a million seasons and still leave the surface of the subject barely scraped with regard to content to draw from—and we are talking about the U.S. alone.

Paycheck to paycheck living has become something of an American cultural phenomena. Perhaps the biggest problem with it is that most times, when massive debts are not present to call attention to the severity of the problem, living from one monthly paycheck to the other looks easy to fix.

You tell yourself that all you need to do is to "reduce your spending, no matter how marginally, next month" and you will be fine. The next time, you raise this issue in the company of some friends, listen to the responses, and marvel at the vague solutions they believe can work. The reality, however, is that when your life is about anxiously looking forward to the next check, you are a financial cripple. You are powerless and are at the mercy of any emergency that may come your way.

Most Americans do not even understand the concept of an emergency fund, let alone having one in place. This is a shocking reality. What happens when you fall seriously ill and the bills start to pile up once you use up your insurance?

Further, if an emergency fund is not in place, it is likely that there is no retirement plan in place either. What happens when you grow too old for your job? Does the next step have to be extremely frugal living, and shortly after, death? Do you have to nag your kids for sustenance when you are too old to work?

All this looks exaggerated and over the top, but remember, every financial decision you make daily has a say on how your financial landscape will look in your 50s, and older. Little things add up to create big things.

Statistics tell defined stories. The US has an average household income of $52,000 or thereabout a year. Only a handful of people are able to save up 5.6% of their annual salary; 76% of all US households and citizens have a difficult time living a normal life if a monthly check is late. In a land where there is so much excess, a land so wealthy that it can afford to put up welfare programs and basketball courts even in the poorest areas of the country, only 14% have an idea of what financial freedom is.

We live in an American culture where spending before thinking and planning is the norm. Most Americans have credit cards. Most Americans swipe these credit cards all the time. Pay comes in at the end of the month and the pay promptly leaves the account in the course of the following month, oftentimes for no good reason at all. Why does this have to be the case?

The purpose of this chapter is to draw attention to the severity of the problem. The purpose of every chapter that follows will be to help you understand how you can unshackle yourself from the problem and start living freely. The next chapter will build on this one; it will show you exactly why you, along with millions upon millions of Americans, struggle to manage your finances in a healthy way.

Before moving onto chapter 2, meditate on this a little.

The true reason why the financial crisis of 2008 was so brutal to so many people was and is simple: because the majority did not understand the concept of saving up for a rainy day. It would be silly to blame the public on 2008's problems, but the homelessness problem would not have been so severe if, leading up to the financial collapse, people had been more responsible with their finances. If a replay of 2008 were to happen this year or the next, what would your circumstances be? Think about this.

Chapter 2: The Financial Habits Of 76% American Households

Let this sink in:

76% of all American households, in one capacity or the other, live from one paycheck to the next. This means that 76%—about 95,927,200 million households going by 2017 figures—of all US citizens would not know what to do if they suddenly lost their jobs or main sources of income.

Considering that most of the world only dreams of earning what the average US household salary earns, it begs the question, why is this? What are the reasons for this financial straitjacket that traps the most privileged citizenry in the world?

1: A Lack Of Personal Financial Understanding

Every day financial matters confuse most people. Here are some confusion examples shared by a lot of the public:

Discernment of assets from liabilities and vice versa is difficult to pull off

Let me put this in the most basic form possible: an asset will put money in your pocket while a liability will take money from your pocket. To build on this, an asset is something you own and that you can turn into cash.

Your car and house qualify as potential assets on the basis that you can turn them into cash. They develop from being potential assets to real assets when you sell them off.

Liabilities include your bills, the balances on your credit card, your loans, as well as other amounts that you owe. In short, liabilities "are what you owe."

A LACK OF FORWARD THINKING WITH REGARD TO SPENDING

This one points to spending with the aim of being happy at that moment (what we call immediate gratification). This sort of thinking makes it very difficult for many people to put together an emergency fund. It is also the leading reason why so many folks cannot help but be in debt.

There is a world of difference between the man who spends $1,000 on the latest PC and the man who saves that $1,000 at a compounded interest rate of 7%. Within 2 years, the latter fellow will have $144.90, plus the $1,000 he originally saved, while the former will have an old PC that has since depreciated.

Too much emphasis on investing in material things

Too many people focus on splurging on expensive, yet depreciating assets such as cars, rather than in things that have long-term value. A degree has infinite value compared to a vehicle of the same value as the degree program tuition.

2: A GENERAL LACK OF RESOURCEFULNESS

That is right; you are not being resourceful!

Most people usually make most of their choices based on convenience. This is why so many people tell lies or cruise at work because these things are easy, cheap options. And speaking of cheap options, there is always a cheaper option available, or a cheaper way of doing things.

You can work double overtime every so often, work two jobs, or you can just work your day job and watch Netflix in the evening instead of working another job. Double overtime or a second job will be taxing on your body and spirit, and you will suffer discomfort. However, the ramifications are awesome: you will have more money in your account, which will allow you to live a higher standard of living if you so choose to.

As Tony Robbins, bestselling author of Money Master the Game: 7 Simple Steps To Financial Freedom, once opined, "A lack of resources is not the cause of failure. Rather, it is the lack of resourcefulness that causes failure."

3: YOU REFUSE TO PAY YOURSELF FIRST, OPTING TO PAY EVERYONE ELSE FIRST

A major reason why you are "poor" may be that you never pay yourself first.

You may be asking yourself, "How do I pay myself first when I am not a business owner?" Well, as a working person, paying yourself first simply means that come rain or shine, a portion of your paycheck has to find its way into your savings account. It does not matter how many payments you have to take care of or if you will have to put up with spaghetti three days in a week, this portion has to go to your savings account every month.

The recommended amount, at least if you want to see substantial results, is 10%. Only after saving this amount (paying yourself first) do you allocate money towards debts and expenses.

Here is a slice of truth for you. A 35-year-old woman driving a modest Morris Minor and eating simple home-cooked meals twice a week, but sitting on a $50,000 savings account she has spent 10 or so years stacking up sleeps better at night compared to the man with a new truck every year and $69 in his savings account.

4: YOU HAVE NO IDEA WHERE YOUR MONEY GOES AFTER COMING IN

You may not be very fond of the nuances and rigors of budgeting. To be honest, very few people beam with joy at the thought of the columns and rows of a budget spreadsheet. Yet, living without a well-defined budget is one of the most foolish things an adult can do.

Quite simply, a budget keeps you on top of every expense. A budget helps you track every penny that leaves your account or wallet. With a budget in place, you cease not knowing where your money is going. With a budget, you KNOW what your outgoing pennies are up to.

Chapter 7 will give you a very thorough walk-through on how to put together a proper budget. At first, it will be difficult to adjust to the new rigors, but remember that pain is the greatest builder. Once you are in control of your money, which happens through your budget, you will ultimately be more in control of your life.

5: You Are Trying Too Hard To Keep up with The Lifestyle And Expectations of Friends, Peers, And Family

It is funny how most people never own up to this while the reality is that just about everyone is doing it. It is very easy to insist on keeping up appearances; we all want to fit in and "not feel lower than those closest to us." However, have you ever considered that your friends may be driving a leased car or have an expensive vacation home whose payments is giving them all sorts of headaches? Perhaps the motivation for the purchases was another friend who had done the same with the same consequences in place for that particular friend.

No matter how much you earn, always strive to live below your means.

Many of us are truly uncomfortable with the prospect of giving up familiar things in life even though they are not as necessary as we make them out to be. An example would be a visit to Starbucks every morning while on our way to work. This book is not suggesting that you cease going to Starbucks, no. This book is merely placing emphasis on the fact that a proper financial state boils down to your priorities. If you feel that coffee is a necessary fuel and as such, Starbucks is a priority, try to make it affordable by reducing other expenses.

Part 2: Stemming The Bleeding

The chapters included in this part of the book cover the steps and strategies to live by in the very first days as you attempt to liberate yourself from paycheck to paycheck living and embark on the journey to financial security and freedom.

If you are living from paycheck to paycheck, every possibility is that you are struggling to keep up with debt payments and normal bills, meaning you do not have much to work with. There is no need to worry; this part of the book will discuss steps you can take to put yourself in a better financial position.

Chapter 3: Automating A 5% Savings Rate and Un-automating Spending

Many finance gurus and experts will insist that you should put away 10-15% of your income. The previous chapter even mentions that an ideal 10% of your monthly income should go to paying yourself (which means you should direct it to a savings account).

There is nothing wrong with this advice; in fact, it is a great starting point. However, if you are truly living from one paycheck to the next, it means putting away 10% let alone 15% is going to be very difficult. If that is the case, start with a savings rate of 5%.

You can do this in multiple ways. You could chat with your employer and request for an automatic withdraw of 5% of your income put into a savings account.

Putting away 5% of your income should not be too hard to accomplish; make sure you automate this 5% income withdrawal. This way, it will happen unconsciously and you will not have to deal with the temptation to spend that 5%.

Once you automate your savings, un-automate spending. To do this, you need to unlearn old money habits.

A great American saying making the rounds says, "The reason why most people are unable to move forward is not necessarily because they are unwilling and incapable of learning new behavior and habits but rather, because they are unwilling or incapable of unlearning old ones."

As far as spending, and living from paycheck to paycheck goes, this saying hits home.

The Hamster Wheel & Reigning Yourself In

We all want to stop the vicious paycheck-to-paycheck cycle. At this point in the guide, you understand that living from one paycheck to the next is akin to riding a hamster wheel: regardless of how much progress you think you have made, you get nowhere. Unfortunately, very few actually ever change their habits to suit their objective of financial freedom.

While it is well and good to make an effort to save for a rainy day, have an emergency fund in place, and ensure adequate coverage in case of a misfortune, how much sense does it make if you impulsively spend the money you have left, and then have to put up with canned spaghetti 6 days out of 7?

Part of being financially free lies in being able to reign yourself; to beat down the temptation to spend on things, no matter how much you think you want them, or how good the offer attached to them is.

The American Culture of Spending Without Thinking

How much have you spent on things like Netflix or video game "packs" this past year? How much have you spent on them the past month alone? Was it truly necessary to order that lovely camouflage-color jacket you saw on eBay, even though you had a similar, but an older version?

The problem with most of us is that we have become so used to "automated" spending that it actually feels weird and even somewhat self-abusive when we reign ourselves in and deny ourselves things that cost money. We spend impulsively, and the costs are all too apparent.

Things like Netflix can easily set you back by $100 a month. If your paycheck is not "all that big" to begin with, you will feel the pinch a lot more. It certainly may feel like you NEED these things; however, 95% of the time, the items you spend money on are not actual needs; you just WANT them.

If you are to liberate yourself financially, you have to start discerning what you need from what you want and then applying spending brakes on the latter, at least for the most part. What is the solution, thus?

You need to "un-automate" your spending. You need to make it a habit to spend only on things that are necessary, at least most of the time. The content below helps you apply this.

How To Stop Impulsive Spending

Here is how to determine what you need from what you want:

1. With the exception of obvious things such as food, shelter, and clothing e, ignore spending money on everything else once the next paycheck comes through. It is simple (albeit not easy) to pull off. Simply seek to handle only necessities.

2. In the space of a month, you will find that for the things you truly need, such as the internet perhaps, you will miss them and their absence will negatively affect your life in one way or the other. The absence of things you only want but do not necessarily need will not really have much of an impact. You may crave them occasionally, yes, but you will be just fine without them. These are the items to avoid splurging on in the future. It is no crime to get yourself a new jacket or pair of shoes, but you do not have to have them every other month.

It is important to note that we all have many necessary expenses automated in nature, just like your monthly spending on video game packs may be. We are talking mortgage payments here, rental payments, car payments, and insurance. This chapter does not recommend that you suspend these ones since they are necessary for your life.

Chapter 4: Paying With Cash Habit and Its Benefits

For best results, combine the recommended exercise in the previous chapter with the recommendations in this one. Doing so will help you incorporate responsible spending habits faster into your life, which will make it easier to end the paycheck to paycheck problem.

The psychological power of insisting on paying cash for everything is all too apparent once you begin doing so. With a swipe of his credit card, a fellow can pay for his groceries. In such a case, the most likely thing is that it will be as unemotional a transaction as they come. You cannot see the money physically leaving your account and you do not feel too invested in the process. However, when you take out five $20 bills and hand them over to the cashiers at your local supermarket, the transaction immediately activates your sense of loss, that in a way that swiping a credit card absolutely ignores.

The next step is to "import" this habit to just about everything else, at the very least for the next 1 month. Keep your credit card away and just use cash for a month. The results will speak volumes to you: there are no surefire guarantees, but it is very likely that you will have a lot more left at the end of that month than was the case previously.

A smart person would persist with this habit for more than one month and seek to mesh it with every other strategy discussed in this book, and even though it is apparent that credit cards are necessary items, and you will need to use them on occasion if only to improve your credit score.

An even smarter person would then take this leftover cash and add it to the stipulated 5% savings rate. It looks absurd but here is the thing. Even a 0.025% increment in savings will bring true financial independence that much closer.

Part 3: Moving Past The Beginner Level & Planting Your Financial Feet On Firm Ground

Now that you have the foundation, a foundation that when followed diligently, will set you on the path to true financial freedom, you are ready to kick things up a notch. The chapters included in this third part of the guide will help usher you through the preliminary stages of financial stability and firmly onto the path to true financial freedom:

Chapter 5: Calculate Your Monthly Cash Flow

Step 1: Examine Your Typical Monthly Bank Statement

Have a good look at your typical monthly bank statement. At the very least, that is the point where it all begins.

Create a spreadsheet document and fill in four columns: Income, Expenses, AOI (Averaged Other Income) and AOE (Averaged Other Expenses). Averaged Other Income will point to other income you may have besides your regular paycheck, while Averaged Other Expenses point to other expenses besides the usual.

Step 2: Start by Focusing on Your Income per Month

Get to know just how much you have in a typical month. Add up income from all your income streams. This will include scholarships, child support, federal benefits, and savings interest. The only income you will not add to this column should be income that does not come on a month-by-month basis. Put this in a separate AOI column.

Step 3: Add up All Monthly Expenses

1. Add up all the money that goes out. This is inclusive of money you direct towards investments and savings.

2. Next, add housing expenses like mortgage, rental payments, and property tax.

3. After you have added these, add your monthly bills such as gas bills, internet bills, cable, water, and sewer bills. ☐

4. Food-related costs should follow such as grocery expenses. ☐

5. If you do not drive to work and prefer to take the subway or taxi, add the amount you spend on transportation.

6. Add amounts you channel towards loan payments as well as insurance and healthcare monies.

7. If you have kids, calculate and add the amounts you use for childcare and tuition.

8. Finally, include the amounts you direct toward clothing, gifts, recreation, and the likes.

9. If an expense is unusual by virtue of being random in nature or large, include it in the AOE column

STEP 4: AVERAGE UNUSUAL CASH FLOW

Determine how much income you have that comes in on a non-monthly basis. For instance, if you get some amount every 3 months for putting in some semester-long shift, include it in.

The next step is to determine how much of such income you make in a year. Going by our example above, you will multiply the semester payments by 4. Proceed to divide the annual amount by 12 so you can get a monthly estimate.

STEP 5: ADD UP POSITIVE CASH FLOW

Add all your income amounts together. This will be your positive cash flow.

STEP 6: CALCULATE THE NEGATIVE CASH FLOW

Add up all your expenses, including the unusual ones. This will be your negative cash flow, the amount that leaves your account, and ultimately your life, on a month-by-month basis.

STEP 7: SUBTRACT THE NEGATIVE CASH FLOW FROM THE POSITIVE CASH FLOW

If the balance has a positive number, you have a positive cash flow and you have money available for investing or directing toward outstanding debts to help clear them faster. If you get a negative balance number, you have a negative cash flow and you need to reverse this.

This section of the book includes chapters that will help you turn your negative cash flow into a positive one.

Chapter 6: Take Back Financial Control - Create A Proper Budget For Financial Organization

Most of us "intend" to save up some money. The savings may not come in every month but there is always that intention to save up frequently. Unfortunately, this often proves consistently impossible.

How many times has a month wound down, only for you to realize on the 30th of the month that you have already spent the money you intended to save? How many times does a month wind down and you are at a loss as to what you actually spent your money on or used it?

If this sounds familiar, it thus follows that your finances are a mess. This chapter will show you how to draw up a proper budget that will pull you out of the financial deep waters.

Here is how to create your budget:

Step 1: Set Some Defined Goals

You probably have an idea of how you would like your finances to have shaped up in a year. It is also likely that you have an idea of how you want your financials to look five years from now. By finances, we do not just mean how large the bank account will look like; things such as a house and a car also factor in.

If you do not have a clear picture of these things, it will be in your own best interests to take some time and figure them out because it makes no sense to save up when you do not know what you are saving up for. If that is the case, you will end up only doing it halfheartedly.

Identify both small and big finance-related goals and then start taking steps that will drive you towards their achievement:

Here are some examples for you:

Emergency savings

You may have some money saved up as emergency savings, but how do you tell if your emergency savings account is healthy enough? For one, if you have not managed to save up enough money to last you 6 months (say if you lost your job or your income checks ceased to roll in every month), it is high time to make building that emergency fund a priority. Emergency funds will be a buffer in case you lose your job or in case something that requires financial input suddenly appears.

Purchasing a car or house

Both a car and a house may be goals you only intend to reach some years or so from now. Nevertheless, to accomplish them, it is necessary that you begin saving up ASAP. Some people get to a point where they think they are ready to buy their car or house but realize they have nowhere near enough money to pay the down payment of their ideal house. The earlier you start your preparations, the better off you will be.

Paying off debt

It is impossible to express yourself as financially successful if you have debt dragging you down. Target the debt payments on your credit card first. Credit cards tend to come with high interest rates, and therefore, the longer you allow them to sit, the more they end up costing you.

The above are just examples. Figure out your goals, write them on a piece of paper, and then pin them somewhere easily visible.

STEP 2: UNDERSTAND HOW MUCH YOU OUGHT TO BE SPENDING

Here is something you already know but have perhaps never seriously meditated on. The fastest route to financial freedom and genuine wealth is by living below your means. The best way to go about living below your means is by having a full picture of what exactly is going on with your money. This allows you to keep your priorities in their place.

There really are no one-size-fits-all rules when it comes to how much you should spend. There are some rules peddled around for sure, but you should not take them as seriously as those selling them insist. However, there are general guidelines that will help you create a budget that helps you reach your financial goals:

You may break your spending into three categories:

1. Fixed costs
2. Goals and savings
3. Flexible spending

Fixed costs: Aim to spend no more than half (50%) your monthly income

Fixed costs will be the bills that, month in month out, tally to roughly the same amounts. The idea is to spend no more than half (50%) of your income on these bills seeing as you will have to channel money toward them anyway. Here are some fixed costs examples:

1. Housing (Ideally, less than 25% of your income should go towards this one. However, 30% is also acceptable. Anything above 30% will only serve to put you in a financial straitjacket)
2. Insurance
3. Utilities
4. Legal obligations (we are talking car payments, debt payments, student loan payments, and the likes)

Goals & savings: Try to get to a point where you consistently put away at least 20% of your income

Failure to prioritize this category is financial suicide because this category pretty much covers all the desirable elements you would like in your life: a car, a house, a debt-free life, and so forth. A major reason why you may be getting to the 30th of the month every month with no money left may be a failure to address this category.

The first part of this book recommends starting with a 5% savings rate. However, this should only be a starting point when your finances are truly a long way off the black. It is far healthier to put away 20% at the end of every month.

Obviously, there will be elements that perhaps make this difficult, such as credit card debt payments, which come with lofty interest rates. In this case, target them first and aggressively too so that you can clear them and thus be able to save more every month.

Flexible spending: 30% of your take-home pay should be the highest you can allow yourself to spend☐

This is inclusive of all expenses incurred from one month to the next. If you can spend only 10% of your take-home amount on this category, you are better off than the person who spends 25%. 30% should be the limit.

This category is inclusive of such things as groceries, shopping, eating out, gas, booze Etc. While things like food and clothes are definitely basic needs, there are ways and means to reduce money spent on food and clothes. Be responsible.

STEP 3: UNDERSTAND JUST HOW MUCH MONEY COMES IN REGULARLY AND HOW MUCH GOES OUT IN THE SAME FASHION

With step 2 done and dusted, you should have a solid idea of how much you spend on what, at least in terms of percentages. It is high time to figure out just how much money is coming in and where you will be channeling it. This is the stage where you will be able to unearth the expenses that are unnecessary, and thus need reduction or complete elimination from your budget.

How much do you actually make?

Before you jump in and declare your employer's quoted figure as your monthly income, pause for a while and consider this: the amount quoted as your annual salary is not actually the amount you make in a year. This often confuses many people once they get their first check.

It works this way: your gross income, which is the amount your boss will swear he/she is paying you, is the total income before the taxman takes his cut, as well as other subtractions that will definitely factor in. Thus, your actual income is not the quoted $35,000 a year. Rather, your actual income is the amount you take home after tax and other deductions.

How much money do you have going out?

The next step is to understand just how much money is going out. Here, we mean how much money you spend in a month. Rather than merely speculate, the best thing to do is to go through last month's spending with a fine toothcomb and consider every expense so that you can understand exactly what you are paying for. Cover everything from house payments to Netflix. Here is a good sequence to follow:

1. Start with recurring bills cum obligations first. We are speaking the likes of housing, insurance, utilities,

cell phone plan, and the likes. Go through each item and note the exact amounts.

2. Follow up by going through all debts payable monthly. This means things like credit card bills, car payments, student loans, and every other debt.

3. Finally, add in all other expenses. It does not matter if you only bought an item the previous month alone, and have never spent a dime on it again; include it too. How much did you spend on takeout last month? How much did you spend on Starbucks lattes? Take note of everything.

4. Your masterstroke (finishing touch) should be to determine just how much you were able to save up. You will do this so that if there is financial mismanagement, it will be all the clearer to see.

This process will not be pretty. However, it will be necessary and will give you have a handle on your spending.

Figure out the points that you will cut costs in

Certainly, the first areas to target should be subscriptions, groceries, shopping, and things like cell phone bills. Here are some strategies you can use to help you cut costs:

Fixed costs:

1. Look for lower insurance rates.
2. Consider cheaper cell phone bills. If this means subscribing to a different service, make the leap.

3. Eliminate all subscriptions you do not use.

Flexible spending:

1. Cut grocery bills by way of coupon apps, shopping at cheaper places, loyalty programs, etc.

STEP 4: BUCKLE DOWN AND CREATE A BUDGET

The less money you direct at expenses in your control, the faster you will move towards being debt-free, saving up, and growing wealthy.

The Process of Budgeting

Take your actual income (minus tax as well as other deductions) and proceed to split it into each spending area. Let us use the example of a $2,000 monthly pay:

Income: $2,000

1. Fixed costs: 50% ($1,000)
2. Financial goals & objectives: 20% ($400)
3. Flexible spending: 30% ($600)

Spread out your paycheck so that it covers each area. This book has recommended paying for all, if not most items, in cash. To maximize order, you can split up your money and place it in different envelopes.

You may be asking, "Is creating a budget truly this simple? I thought I had to work with endless spreadsheet documents?"

Well, you may have to work with spreadsheet documents eventually. However, after taking steps 1, 2, and 3, the budget creation process becomes incredibly simple since you are not trying to figure anything out anymore, and are simply allocating funds to different expense categories.

Chapter 7: Identify & Proceed To Cut Off The Waste In Your Budget

Your lifestyle is unique to you, and it may be that you spend unnecessary amounts on the most unconventional things. However, it is far more likely that the bulk of the money wasted is on the usual suspects such as entertainment, treats, expensive toys, and the likes.

This chapter will suggest several courses of action to take based on these usual suspects.

Cut Your Entertainment Budget

You may have realized it—or you perhaps have not—but entertainment usually takes one of the largest chunks of a monthly budget. You may think this cannot be true, at least on your part, until you factor in just how large the entertainment category is.

It covers just about everything from weekends out to paper subscriptions and even your gym membership. If your cash flow balance is in the high negatives and you seriously need to trim your spending, focus first on this category.

For instance, the average American spends at least $100 on cable subscription; consider cutting this expense. If it is too hard to just cut it and forget about it, consider replacing it with a much cheaper subscription.

If you and your friends have a tradition of visiting every nightclub in the city on payday and spending money on drinks, consider dropping this habit or settling for less costly options. Rather than spending amounts on hardcover books, consider getting their Kindle equivalent or visiting the local library. When it comes to trimming your entertainment expenses, you have a million and one options.

CONSIDER TRIMMING TRANSPORT COSTS

Very few people ever realize that their bursts of unplanned travel badly drain their wallets. It is even worse when you insist on driving to each new place. Public transportation may not seem like a glamorous option but it is a very effective way of keeping travel costs low.

CUT DOWN ON SPECIAL TREATS

By special treats, we mean the likes of tacos, lattes, etc. If you must have coffee in the morning, it is smarter to brew some before work at home rather than spending an accumulated fortune every year on Starbucks lattes. Your daily $3 latte looks like nothing, but this is nearly $100 a month. $100 a month in savings is not such a small amount? This is not to say that you should not treat yourself occasionally. The idea is to keep the money you spend on treats reasonable.

CHAPTER 8: SEEK TO REDUCE YOUR OVERALL SPENDING

The previous chapter offered suggestions on how you can do away with unnecessary expenses. This chapter will show you how to cut back on your spending, even when you are doing so on necessary items. Being financially smart in this way is what will truly give you an edge over everybody else and help you accomplish financial freedom quickly.

CHANNEL ANY BONUSES INTO SAVINGS

Even as far back as the 60s, as depicted by the show "Mad Men," it has always seemed "cool" to splash your bonus on something extravagant like an impromptu trip or an expensive jacket. There is no harm in enjoying life, but it is far more prudent to put your bonus into your savings or at least use it to help clear some debt. By the way, a bonus is not just the amount your boss pushes your way at the end of the year. That $20 you find in your jacket pocket qualifies as a bonus too.

MAKE YOUR MEALS AT HOME

It is tough to summon the energy required to whip up a meal after a long working day. The best starting point is a twice-a-week cooking routine. You can then build up from there. Home cooking is usually a lot cheaper than eating out all the time and it helps you eat a lot healthier as well.

GO GROCERY SHOPPING WHEN FULL

Have you ever gone grocery shopping on a hungry belly? The temptation to buy more than you need is almost overwhelming. Therefore, ensure you go shopping when full.

HAVE A LIST AND SET A SHOPPING LIMIT

Make the decision to cut out all impulsive spending from now on. There are times when you will come across something so appealing that you immediately want to have it. If you come across an expensive scarf while at the mall, rather than whip out your credit card, wait 3 days to a week and see if it still dominates your thoughts. If it still does, then this wait period/time will have given you the time to check for cheaper options online.

CANCEL MEMBERSHIPS TO CLUBS & ENTERTAINMENT BILLS

Undoubtedly, there are certain club memberships you should keep especially if they enrich your life and you regularly attend meetings and events. However, there is no sense in directing money toward a gym membership you never use. Why subscribe to cable TV when you spend 90% of your movie time watching Netflix?

Chapter 9: Pay Off Debts

Pay off your debts one after the other until you clear them all

Quite simply put, debt makes you a slave for as long as it exists. The strategies in this book are top class and even then, following them to the letter while straddling debts will be a lot like trying to carry water in a basket: you will make little progress if any. Start taking your debts very seriously for you will never truly be comfortable with debt in your life.

To establish true financial freedom, one of your foremost priorities should be to eliminate all debt and start living debt-free. This chapter will provide strategies that will make completing your debt payments easier and simpler too.

START BY SETTING A CLEAR DEBT PAYMENT GOAL

A goal includes many factors inclusive of these ones: it is necessary to spell the goal out in clear, specific terms. You have to acknowledge just how taxing it will be to get to the goal and there has to be a defined deadline. Your debt payment goal should seek to cover at least all of the above. Seek to understand the sheer size of your debt, which may require you to arm yourself with a pen and create some lists.

With this in mind, make up your mind on just when you would like all your debts cleared. It may not be so straightforward to do this, especially if you have mortgage and vehicle payments to make, but for the rest of the debts, such as credit card debt, it should not be too complicated to determine a completion date.

Going out and setting a date of debt completion adds a lot of purpose to your goal. It is easier to follow a strict budget when you know your goal is time-bound.

"Freeze" Your Credit Cards

To give yourself a true chance at being debt-free, you need to do something about your credit cards. Conventional advice says you need discipline when it comes to whipping out your credit cards for purchases. This book says you should remove your credit cards from your wallet every time you leave the house. This will eliminate any chance of temptation.

Do you feel as though this is a bit much? Try this. If your credit card payments are severely dragging you down, freeze your credit cards until you have completed all outstanding payments. Not only will living a credit card-free life for a while help you gain better control of your finances, it will also teach you about what is and is not a necessary expense.

List Down and Prioritize All Debts

It will benefit you greatly to create a list of all debts, and then figure out which debts are most important to clear early or pay off with utmost promptness. Here is a simplistic tip for you. Vehicle payments and mortgage payments should be at the top of the importance list, and with good reason: you likely need your vehicle to get to your job, and your house is a necessity: you live in it.

Still, your priorities will be unique for the most part. Perhaps you have some high-interest payments you want to clear up quickly or a payday loan you would love to pay up. Decide which payments to pay off early and do your best to ensure you follow your plan.

Utilize "The Most Popular Way to Get Out of Credit Card Debt"

This method calls on you to follow a strategic routine to deal with credit card debt. Firstly, you will pay off debts with fixed monthly payments (think mortgage payments, vehicle payments, and the likes), seeing as these are by far the most necessary payments to handle.

After taking care of these, make the smallest payment required on your credit cards, which have the lowest interest rates and seek to maximize payments on those credit cards that have high rates of interest. Once you have completely done away with a high-interest payment, channel your attention to the debt payment with the next-highest interest rate. Not only is this a great strategy to help you pay off debt fast, you will also save considerable chunks of money along the way.

The Snowball Debt Reduction Strategy

Rather than focus aggressively on payments with the highest interest rates, this method calls for you to focus on the smallest credit card payments first and then work your way up. If anything, it will likely have a potent psychological effect on you; knowing that you have completed a payment will give you a great psychological boost.

Here is how to apply this method:

1. Any extra money that comes your way should promptly go toward paying off the smallest balance at the time. Here, ignore interest rates and simply look to see the smallest balance before concentrating your attention on it.

2. Once you have completed a payment set, rather than put away (in savings) the amount you were using to pay off the debt, use it to pay down the next-smallest balance. Certainly, you should stick to the policy of channeling all extra monies toward paying down the debt.

3. The monthly payments you free up as you knock off debt payment after debt payment will make it a lot easier to deal with the progressively bigger debts you turn your attention to. By doing this, you will create a snowball effect.

PART 4: DOING MORE TO BE MORE:

It is a great strategy to attempt to make your current income go further and last longer. However, it is undeniable that things will be even better if you bring in more income. At the very least, it will be easier to draw up a budget and save up. The strategies in this section of the book will focus on adding to your income and in so doing, getting you closer to financial freedom.

Chapter 10: Strategies To Employ To Earn More Money And Get Closer To Financial Freedom

This chapter will focus on steps you can take to increase your income and gain financial freedom

Begin A Small Side Hustle

When it comes to your side gig, the perfect situation is if you set it up in a way that allows you to work on it during your free hours because in this way, it will not interfere with your day job.

There are dozens of ways you can begin to earn additional money. The unwritten rule for most of these strategies is that the beginning will always be slow but by and by, the gig will grow and bring in greater returns as more and more people buy into it.

A great example of such a side gig is starting a YouTube channel. YouTube channels will usually start out slowly unless you are already a celebrity who has primed potential viewers to expect your channel. However, as you produce more videos, your stuff will start to show up more often on search results, leading to subscribers. The more views you get, the easier it is to draw in advertisers, ultimately leading to some income.

A YouTube channel will grow organically and eventually become a force but fair warning, it may take some time. The same is true for most online content forms of side hustles such as blogging and creating landing pages.

Here are other side gig examples for you:

1. Providing a service you are skilled in
2. Selling a rare or distinct product in your area
3. Providing personalized expertise in niche areas such as year-round lawn maintenance for people in your area.

MAKE YOURSELF READY FOR A BETTER JOB

Have you considered that you may be too skilled for your current or old job? It really may be time to move on to something better as far as your career goes. It could be that your skills are beyond the demands and responsibilities of your current job and the truth is that you could do a lot better if you tried.

Most people make the mistake of prioritizing their job comfort over all other career aspects, but this often means they end up underpaid and underachieving, relative to their skill set. Are you one of these people?

To make a career improvement, you need to take certain steps, the first of which is rather obvious: figuring out exactly what the next step is. Where should you steer your career? Are you simply looking to improve your job level, to move from Salesman class B to class A? Are you looking to replace your current boss once she moves to a different position?

Once you have decided where you want to go, evaluate the requirements of the new job. Which ones can you already boast to have? More importantly, which ones do you not have? Once you believe you meet the necessary requirements, it will be time to begin seeking your promotion.

CONSIDER SWITCHING ORGANIZATIONS

This one directly relates to the previous strategy. It is quite likely that you will find yourself stuck in limbo and unable to make progress in your current organization. Perhaps your boss refuses to see the value you bring, and will thus neither give you a raise nor consider promoting you. It could be that there is no defined path to make your way up the company ladder. It could well be that the job atmosphere in your current organization is too toxic. Perhaps, the pay rate is lower than what a person of your skill could get in another organization.

If any of the situations listed are all too common in your situation, it may be time to switch organizations. You stand to gain far more than you could potentially lose.

It is vital to understand that this can take time. You will have to find positions that are suitable to your skill set and in a suitable location. You will then have to apply for these jobs and then battle other applicants for the job.

Your first step will be the actual job hunt. Are there organizations similar to yours close by? Are there any jobs like yours available? What does the paycheck look like? Are there any job requirements in place that you perhaps do not meet? Make your research thoroughly before you make a move. Most importantly, do not hand in your letter of resignation before you have snagged a new job.

BECOME CERTIFIED

This may not be news to you but we will include it anyway: most career paths and jobs appreciate employees who take the time to accrue certification in various areas and topics. The employers even go out of their way to reward such people. The certifications do not even have to be overly impressive. Earning simple Oracle database certifications will often be enough to see you become automatically eligible for pay increases or even a promotion.

Does your job have pay benefits in the event that you earn certifications? Would a set of newly earned certifications improve your appeal as far as promotion potential goes? If you are not sure about the answers to these questions, research, speak to your colleagues or perhaps have a five-minute chat with HR.

Certainly, you have to go out of your way to earn these certifications. The good news is that the career world has come a long way, and many certifications are available online or in evening classes close by.

It will call for you to use some funds to earn these certifications but in truth, it will be worth it. A pay rise or even a job promotion will fast track you toward financial freedom.

TAKE UP A PART-TIME JOB

A part-time job gives you the opportunity to convert free time into extra money.

All you need to do is hunt around a bit. Most communities, especially in the U.S., have an abundance of part-time jobs available. There are all forms of part-time gigs; some part-time gigs are entry level while some will require that you use your job skills so that it almost appears as though you are merely working overtime. If you are not too specific, there are limitless options for you. You could end up whipping up lattes or providing security.

Of all the strategies covered in this part of the book, this strategy will be the most direct, least demanding way to generate some extra cash. Most part-time jobs like to hire quickly. Thus, if you act immediately, you could have an extra income in less than one month.

With regard to part-time jobs, the best thing you could do is to understand that they are rarely ever flexible. If a part-time job clashes in any way or form with your day job or something that is very important to you, graciously turn it down regardless of how appealing it is. You could stubbornly insist on taking it up and even succeed on some level, but the extra tension returns that are lower than your day job are not really worth it. Try to get a part-time job that allows you to do your day job if your day job is important.

TAKE ON A COUPLE OF CASUAL INCOME EARNERS

Countless websites out there offer you a chance to earn a couple of dollars for doing very light duties or work that you can accomplish while watching reruns of your favorite show. Usually, the tasks involve undemanding activities such as filling out online surveys or determining which picture, out of a set of them, contains a snooker 8 ball. Some of these tasks require a bit of skill but even then, they do not really stretch you: the skill level they demand will rarely ever go above decent competence in doing simple Photoshop images.

If you cannot be bothered with casual income earners that demand skill and would love to keep it simple, start with websites like www.mechanicalturk.com. With Mechanical Turk, you will choose amongst a range of simplistic chores such as writing very short, reasonably structured bits. You can also write simple three-line reviews of a product. If you are consistent, you will definitely earn a healthy amount.

If you would love to flex your technical skills, you can start with a site like Fiverr www.fiverr.com). The bulk of tasks on this platform favor application of swiftly executed programming skills or Photoshop skills. Again, you will not need to dedicate more than a few minutes at a time, especially if you have a degree of competence.

If you have a high and diversified skill level, a site like www.upwork.com will be well suited for you. You stand to earn more for taking on more complicated tasks. up work has all sorts of freelancing jobs that will allow you to exercise your technical skills in your spare time.

ENGAGE YOUR BOSS IN A SERIOUS CHAT

Why is such a simplistic piece of advice here? Well, a lot of the time, the most direct things give the best results. With regard to achieving financial freedom, this is especially true. Oftentimes, your boss is the best, most direct route to a pay bump. Your boss has the power to authorize a raise, meaning you are subject to more income for doing the same tasks you are already familiar with and doing. You can try this; and no, being afraid of the boss or "not wanting to ruffle feathers" are simply not good enough reason.

Like most things that require seriousness, these conversations tend to roll along best when you have taken the time to prepare for them. Having a potent case to present to your boss, and showing you have taken the time to think through, along with supportive evidence, will help convince your boss to offer you a pay bump.

How do you prepare? Well, you need to find a quiet place, sit down, and review all your achievements at work. Try and especially look out for the more significant ones. What things have you done that set you apart from the other employees? What achievements make you more deserving of a pay rise? If it is difficult to come up with answers to these questions, perhaps it is time to buckle down and work harder. If you cannot find any real reason why you deserve a pay bump, your boss will have no real reason to offer you one.

LEVERAGE WHAT YOU HAVE TO EARN MORE INCOME

You could say this one is a variation of the side gig strategy, and you would not really be wrong. However, this is a lot more flexible, in comparison to a side gig, and depending on how aggressive you are, you can earn a decent amount of income. Here, you leverage what you have, or what you deeply understand, and via trading, buying and selling, earn some dollars.

Take this real-life example. A person from Europe makes a few trips to the U.S. every year. He is a big soccer fan, and he understands that soccer, while certainly relevant on the American sports scene, is nowhere near as huge as it is in Europe. In America, people are simply not as indoctrinated in the ways of soccer as they are in Europe. Thus, at stores, it is common to see rare vintage soccer jerseys go for a paltry $10.

The person is happy to buy the jersey for $10, knowing that he will easily be able to sell it for upwards of $100 once he gets back home. It is a rare piece after all, and unlike modern jerseys that are easy to find at any decent sports store, finding one like it anywhere is really a matter of luck.

This is just but one example, and you do not need to fly out of the country. Simply look for something you have a deep understanding of and figure out how to trade it for profits. It could be that you are quite knowledgeable on vintage board games. Whenever you are at a store, look out for a board game that has decent value on the secondary market. The store will be happy to let you have it for a small amount. You can then seek to trade it on the secondary market and earn a lot more than you spent on it.

Conclusion

We have come to the end of the book. Thank you for reading and congratulations on reading until the end.

You may have noticed one consistent theme all through this guide: to become financially independent, it is paramount that you be proactive.

It is not enough to hope for better things. You need to sacrifice and seek to make what you have gone a long way. With that said, adopting any strategy in this book will be enough to see you make significant progress. Combining all the strategies in this book will definitely see you accomplish financial freedom, and quickly too.

Ask yourself this, "why can't I be financially free like others surely are?" Follow this up with buckling down and working toward your goal. It may take time to arrive there, but you will eventually get there if you take consistent action towards getting there.

If you found the book valuable, can you recommend it to others? One way to do that is to post a review on Amazon.

Thank you and good luck!

How to Deal with Debt Collectors and Win Every Time How To Beat Them at Their Own Game

ERNIE BRAVEBOY

INTRODUCTION

I want to thank you and congratulate you for buying the book, *"How to Deal with Debt Collectors and Win Every Time How To Beat Them at Their Own Game"*.

This book has actionable information on how to deal with debt collectors and win every time.

If debt collectors have ever come after you, you understand that debt collection is one of the most frightening experiences ever.

Debt collectors are like predators who are always circling around, waiting for a chance to pounce on their prey. Hence, they will use any tricks and techniques to get you to pay up. Sometimes they will threaten you and at other times, they may harass you and make you uncomfortable, all in the bid to get you to rush off to pay whatever bills they claim you owe.

There are several ways to beat debt collectors at their game. Many of the techniques they use to intimidate you are illegal and even when they use legal strategies, there are legal ways to get them off your back.

This book explores techniques and strategies you can use to get debt collectors off your back, erase your debts, and win against them in court if they decide to sue you. This book is a no-fluff, straight to the point, a systematic guide with proven techniques other debtors have used to beat debt collectors at their own game.

HOW TO DEAL WITH DEBT COLLECTORS

Let us dig in.

Thanks again for buying this book. I hope you enjoy it!

ERNIE BRAVEBOY

© Copyright 2018 by Ernie Braveboy - All rights reserved.

This document is geared towards providing exact and reliable information in regards to the topic and issue covered. The publication is sold with the idea that the publisher is not required to render accounting, officially permitted, or otherwise, qualified services. If advice is necessary, legal or professional, a practiced individual in the profession should be ordered.

- From a Declaration of Principles which was accepted and approved equally by a Committee of the American Bar Association and a Committee of Publishers and Associations.

In no way is it legal to reproduce, duplicate, or transmit any part of this document by either electronic means or in printed format. Recording of this publication is strictly prohibited and any storage of this document is not allowed unless with written permission from the publisher. All rights reserved.

The information provided herein is stated to be truthful and consistent, in that any liability, in terms of inattention or otherwise, by any usage or abuse of any policies, processes, or directions contained within is the solitary and utter responsibility of the recipient reader. Under no circumstances will any legal responsibility or blame be held against the publisher for any reparation, damages, or monetary loss due to the information herein, either directly or indirectly.

Respective authors own all copyrights not held by the publisher.

The information herein is offered for informational purposes solely and is universal as so. The presentation of the information is without a contract or any type of guarantee assurance.

The trademarks that are used are without any consent, and the publication of the trademark is without permission or backing by the trademark owner. All trademarks and brands within this book are for clarifying purposes only and are the owned by the owners themselves, not affiliated with this document.

Chapter 1: How Debt Collection Agencies Work

The first step towards successfully getting debt collectors off your back is to know whom they really are and how they work.

In most cases, debt collectors are representatives of debt collection agencies. However, some debt collection agencies operate individually. Debt collectors act as intermediaries between debtors and creditors. Their job is to help organizations like banks, credit card companies, car dealerships, student loan issuers, utility companies and other creditors to recover delinquent debts from debtors.

Delinquent debts are debts that are at least 60 days past due. They collect the debts and then remit them to the creditor after deducting their commission, which could range from 25-45% of the recovered debt.

Other types of debt collection agencies act as debt buyers. They purchase debts at a discount after a bidding process. For instance, if you owe a company $2,000, a debt buyer may purchase the debt for about $100 and then from there, they take over the debt fully and begin to pursue the debtor to pay up. If they are lucky enough to get the debtor to pay $2,000 or something close, they will make a profit of around $1,900, which is why they can sometimes be very aggressive.

Sometimes, debt collection agencies will try to negotiate a settlement amount with the debtor and encourage the debtor to pay a lesser amount than owed as a final settlement of the debt. Should the debtor refuse to make payments, debt collection agents may decide to file a lawsuit and get a court injunction that will force the debtor to pay up what they owe.

Why Businesses Use Debt Collectors

You must be wondering why your creditors will not come after you themselves but choose to use the services of debt collection agencies or even sell your debts to them instead.

Well, here is why:

1. They can be paid a good portion of the money owed to them from the debt collection agency and thus avoid expensive lawsuits. When businesses use debt collection agents, they can focus on their businesses and avoid the stress and expenses that come with debt collection.

2. Debt collectors are very skilled and efficient at recovering debts. They know the right things to say to get money out of debtors. They also have software and tools that they use to differentiate debtors who cannot pay up because they are in financial distress, and debtors who can afford to pay the debts—debt collectors usually go after the latter category since there is a better chance of getting their money from these set of people.

How Debt Collection Agencies Operate

As soon as they take up the job of recovering debts from you, they scrape up all the details they can find about you and then either call you or send you a letter to inform you about the debt as a way to try to convince you to pay up.

Usually, debt collectors have sophisticated software and tools they use to find information about you including your residential address and your phone numbers. At other times, they may look into your bank accounts and other assets you own to see if you can afford to repay the debts.

If after trying to convince you to pay, you do not pay up, debt collectors will usually pursue two courses of actions:

1: REPORT TO CREDIT BUREAUS

Debt collectors understand that reporting your debts to the credit bureaus will hurt your credit score, which may pose some financial problems for you in the future especially when you need to obtain credit from other businesses, which is why if you refuse to pay up, they report the debt to the credit bureaus.

2: OBTAIN A COURT JUDGMENT

A debt collector cannot force you to pay what you owe so what they do is to take the case to court and obtain a judgment against you. If they succeed in court, the court will grant them the right to garnish your wages, which means legally deducting what you owe from your salary account. The court may also give them permission to place a lien on your assets or force a sale in order to recover the debts.

HOW TO DEAL WITH DEBT COLLECTORS

One of the important things you must know when dealing with debt collectors is your rights as a debtor. There are laws that protect you as a debtor. You can use these laws as tools to get debt collectors off your back.

The next chapter discusses these laws in-depth:

Chapter 2: What Debt Collection Agencies are Not Allowed to Do

Debt collectors are bound by (and operated under) the FDCPA (Fair Debt Collection Practices Act).

The FDCPA is a federal law that specifies what different debt collectors are allowed to do and what they are not allowed to do as they pursue loan recovery. The United States Federal Government put the law in place to keep debt collection agencies from resorting to desperate, deceptive, and unfair measures to recover debts.

The FDCPA law does not apply to business debts; it only applies to personal or family debts such as utility bills, student loans, medical debts, mortgages, credit card bills, and so on. Another thing you must take note of is that this law only applies to debt collection agencies or debt buyers.

If you owe American Express for instance, and someone who works with AMEX contacts you about your debts, the FDCPA law does not apply to them although the government also expects them to be reasonable with their debt collection procedures too. This law applies to third-party debt collectors whose major business is collecting debts for profits.

What They Cannot Do

The law stipulates that third-party debt collectors cannot:

HOW TO DEAL WITH DEBT COLLECTORS

1: Contact you at an Unusual Time or Place

The law requires debt collectors to respect boundaries: they cannot call you whenever and however they like.

The FDCPA law specifies that debt collectors can only call debtors within the hours of 8 am and 9 pm. This means that they cannot call you before 8 am in the morning or after 9 pm in the evening.

In addition, if a debt collector knows that you cannot receive calls during working hours (you can write them an official letter informing them of this), the law keeps them from calling you while you are at work.

2: Contact You after You Refer them to Your Attorney

Once you have a lawyer and tell the debt collector to talk to your attorney, the law dictates that a debt collector CANNOT communicate with you. All further communications should be with your lawyer instead.

3: Harass You

Under no circumstance should a debt collector harass you whether by letter or over the phone. If they do so, you can report them for harassment and they could get in serious trouble for doing so. Harassment has led to bans of many debt collection agencies.

4: Contact You after You Instruct Them to Stop

You can write a letter to a debt collector instructing them to stop contacting you.

This letter is called a **'cease and desist'** letter and as soon as a debt collector gets the letter, they are no longer allowed to contact you about debt repayments except to inform you that they will be taking legal actions against you like reporting you to the credit bureau or taking you to court.

5: Talk to Other People about the Debt You Owe

The law keeps debt collectors from using embarrassment as a debt collection strategy: it keeps them from talking to your employer about your debts except where there is a court injunction against you.

The law keeps them from talking to friends, family, or anybody else but you about your debts. Similarly, it keeps them from publishing your name if you refuse to pay up.

6: Contact You about Debts That Have Passed the Statute of Limitation

This is something you must pay very keen attention to. As soon as a debt collector contacts you, you must investigate the debt the collection agency is talking about to confirm that it has not passed the statute of limitation.

Typically, a debt collector cannot contact you after a debt has passed a period specified by law. This period differs from one state to another but it is usually between 4 and 7 years.

Confirm the statute of limitation for your state and if the time has lapsed, simply tell the debt collector to stop calling you and they will desist.

7: Lie about What You Owe

Debt collectors should do their due diligence properly before they start contacting you: the Fair Debt Collection Practices Act states that they cannot contact you about debts you do not owe or lie about what you owe.

8: Make False or Bogus Claims or Threats

A debt collector cannot threaten to arrest you or place a lien on your assets except in instances where they have obtained court injunctions to do so. Threatening you as a technique to get you into panic mode so that you can pay up is illegal.

9: Lie That They Represent the Company You Owe

Another trick that debt collectors use is to lie that they are direct representatives of the company you owe. They understand their limits as debt collectors, and would sometimes try to pretend that they are not debt collectors. This is illegal and you can report or sue them for this.

10: Provide False Credit Information to Credit Bureaus

If a debt collector is going to report you to a credit bureau, then he/she had better be sure you owe that debt and have the necessary evidence to back it up. If they do not, you can have them remove it from your credit report.

11: Send You False Court or Official Documents

Another tactic debt collectors and collection agencies use is that of sending you some official documents claiming they are court injunctions. They do this to get you to panic so that you can pay up very fast. Investigate any document they send you and if you discover that they are false, you can take legal actions against them.

12: Garnish the Following Assets after a Lawsuit

Even if a debt collector obtains a court injunction against you that allows them to forcefully collect their debts, they cannot touch some assets like:

1. Your social security benefits
2. Death and disability benefits
3. Military annuities and survivor's benefits
4. Veteran benefits
5. Student assistant
6. Civil service and federal retirement benefits
7. Disability benefits
8. Supplemental security income

13: Try to Collect Interest or Charges on the Debts

Lastly, debt collectors cannot charge interests, late payment charges, or other penalties on what you owe.

Let's now discuss how to report debt collection agencies for the above wrongdoings.

HOW TO REPORT DEBT COLLECTION AGENTS FOR HARASSMENT OR UNFAIR PRACTICES

If a debt collector is harassing you or has done any of the things not legally allowed by the Fair Debt Collection Practices Act, you should immediately inform them that the law in place keeps them from doing that, and inform them that you will be taking legal actions against them for it.

They will usually back off when you inform them that you will be suing them: no debt collector wants to "catch a case" for a $500 debt or have their businesses sanctioned for that. When you inform them that you will be suing them for malpractice or harassment, they will usually back off.

You could also take some other actions to show them that you are willing to walk the talk. You can:

- **Report them to the Consumer Financial Protection Bureau (CFPB)**

If the debt collector violates any of the FDCPA laws mentioned above, you can file a complaint against them with the Consumer Financial Protection Bureau (CFPB). Make sure you get the name of the debt collector and their company's names and report them to CFPB so that the bureau can impose legal sanctions against that debt collector.

- **Report them to the Federal Trade Commission**

You can also file a complaint against the debt collection agent with the Federal Trade Commission (FTC). FTC is an independent government agency that upholds debt collection laws and can take actions against erring debt collection agents.

- **Report them to The State Attorney General**

Some states have specific laws guiding debt collection. You can find out what your state's debt collection laws are; if it turns out that the debt collection agent has violated any of these laws, you can report them to the office of your state's attorney general so that the office can take legal actions against the debt collector.

- **Report to the Better Business Bureau**

Lastly, you can report the debt collection business or agency to the Better Business Bureau (BBB) to discourage businesses from using their services as debt collection agents.

With that in mind, let's now narrow the discussion down to when the debt collector plays by the rules. How do you deal with the situation? That's what we will be discussing next.

Chapter 3: What to Do When a Debt Collector Contacts You

Usually, many debt collectors will leave you alone when they find out that you are not willing to cooperate.

Debt collectors would rather spend their time and resources pursuing ignorant and fearful debtors than going after one who seems smart and ready to go toe to toe with them.

In addition, the costs of pursuing legal action are sometimes not worth it for debt collectors. Can you imagine taking a $200 debt case to court? It is not cost effective for them and is a waste of their time and resources and so, **to beat debt collectors**, you must first **show them that you fully understand debt collection laws and that you are not scared of going to court.** Many of them will back off after this.

Your first line of defense against debt collection agents is to know how to respond to them, and how to communicate with them properly. You have to say the right things and respond the right way to avoid indicting yourself or saying the wrong things that the debt collector can use against you in a court of law.

Let us now discuss how to respond to debt collection agents when they call you up or send you a mail/letter requesting you make payments.

How to Respond to Debt Collection Agents on Phone

Here is how to respond to debt collectors who contact you via phone:

1: Always be Alert and Ask Smart Questions

Do not let them catch you off guard. You must always anticipate their calls and be ready to ask the right questions.

Sometimes, a debt collection agent may not have your current address; that means such a debt collection agent cannot send you any letters. That is one of the many ways to beat them at their game: because the law requires them to send you an official letter about what you owe within five days of contacting you.

If they do not have your address, there is no way to send this letter; however, if you let them catch you off-guard, they may cleverly sweet-talk you into giving them this information before you know what is happening. Therefore, you need to be 'uptight' when it comes to debt collection agents and avoid saying too much to them.

When they call, start by asking the following questions:

1. What is your name?
2. What is the name of the debt collection agency you represent?
3. What is the official address of the debt collection agency?
4. What is the name of the creditor?

5. How much does the creditor claim I owe? It is important to use the word 'claim' here because if you say something like "How much do I owe?" It means you are already agreeing up to the debt, something they can use against you in a court of law.

During this conversation, you want to get as much detail from the collector as possible while neglecting to give any information about yourself or your finances.

The debt collector may try to sound authoritative or use other intimidating or scare tactics to get you to give up more than you are willing to; think of a debt collector as a toothless dog because really, they cannot do anything to you except when the court orders it.

Record the Conversation

As soon as a debt collector calls and introduces him or herself, you should immediately inform the debt collector on the other end of the line that you will start recording the conversation and then press the record button on your phone to get all your conversation on record. If your phone does not come with the call-recording feature, you can buy a tape recorder and use it to record the calls instead— this means you have to put the phone on loudspeaker.

We have many innovative tape recorders that you can use to record phone conversations. The Olympus VN-7600PC is a very good product for this purpose; you can easily get it from online stores like Best Buy or Amazon for around $100.

You should also record any other conversations you have with the debt collector after that. If the debt collector leaves you a voicemail, make sure you keep a record of the voicemails sent to you. However, you must note that recording conversations on phone is illegal in some states so make sure you are aware of the position of the law on this in your state.

If it is illegal to record phone conversations in your state, avoid communicating with the debt collector on phone; instead, tell the debt collector to send you a letter instead. This will help you keep correspondences on the conversation in a legally acceptable way.

In states where it is illegal to record phone conversations, you can also use recorded voicemails in your defense.

WHY YOU SHOULD RECORD YOUR CONVERSATIONS WITH A DEBT COLLECTOR

Because any errors or misconduct—no matter how slight—by the debt collector can get you off the hook, and get your debt erased if the evidence is admitted in court. The law is not usually on the side of debt collectors who break the law while attempting to recover debts.

In the case of FOTI versus NCO FINANCIAL SYSTEMS INC., the court let the defendant off the hook because the debt collector failed to leave sufficient information that would help the defendant identify them as a debt collection agency.

HOW TO DEAL WITH DEBT COLLECTORS

Personally, I think that the defendant might have been avoiding the debt collector's calls and so the debt collector decided to leave him a series of voicemails and then took him to court after some time. However, once in court, the court ruled that there was no way the debtor could have known that NCO Financial Systems was a debt collection agency because the caller did not specifically use the word "debt collector or debt collection agency" in the voicemail left.

This is just one example of how keeping correspondences, especially phone calls and letters from debt collection agencies, can help your case against the debt collector.

ASK THE DEBT COLLECTOR TO SEND YOU AN OFFICIAL LETTER

After asking the necessary questions, tell the debt collector to send you a letter to that effect. Tell them you really have no idea of the debt they are talking about, and that they should send you more details.

Now, this is one loophole: many debt collectors, especially debt buyers, do not have sufficient information about the debt you owe. Some will not even have your house address or know where to address the letter. There is a chance that they will want to get information from you especially your address. You should avoid giving it to them. You should simply tell them that since they claim you owe them, they should have all of this information in their records.

After you make this demand, the law mandates that the debt collector send you a debt validation letter within 5 days. The debt collector should then not contact you about the debt again until they have sent you this letter, and they must send the letter within 5 days.

Sample Phone Call Transcript to use with Debt Collectors

To make things super easy for you, I have come up with a sample phone call transcript you can use with debt collectors.

We shall outline two scripts you can use in different scenarios:

1st Script: If you are Not Sure about the Debt

Debt Collector: "Hello, can I speak to Charlie/ is this Charlie?"

Charlie: "Who am I speaking with please?"

NOTE: At this stage, the law states that the debt collector must identify himself or herself as a debt collection agent.

Debt Collector: "My name is Alex, a debt collector/collector from Dash Collections, the Collection agency representing Cups and Spoons Limited on your outstanding balance of $2,500. I need to know if you are ready to take care of the past due bill at this time."

Charlie: "Sir, "I'm going to be recording this conversation, please kindly hold on while I turn on my recording device."

HOW TO DEAL WITH DEBT COLLECTORS

NOTE: Use this pause to not only turn on your recorder, which you should do, but also take some time to ponder on the debt and try to remember if the statute of limitations on the debt has expired or otherwise- remember we talked about the statute of limitations earlier.

If you are unsure, return to the call.

Charlie: Ask the following questions so that you can get it on record:

1. What is your name?
2. What is the name of the debt collection agency you represent?
3. What is the official address of the debt collection agency?
4. What is the name of the creditor?
5. How much does the creditor claim I owe?

Charlie: "Please kindly confirm, are Cups and Spoons Limited your employer?"

NOTE: What you are trying to do here is to establish if the debt has been sold or handed over to a debt buyer/debt collection agency. Remember, I said earlier that the FDCPA laws do not apply to debt collectors employed directly by the creditor. Before you go ahead, you must establish that the caller is truly a debt collector. If the caller is a debt buyer and you do not wish to pay the debt, you can simply go on and say.

Charlie: "I am unable to communicate with debt collectors who are not employees or direct representatives of an acclaimed creditor. Please kindly give me your address so that I can send you a cease and desist letter in accordance with the FDCPA rules. I am also revoking any permission you have to call me at any number so please make this your last call to me."

2ND SCRIPT: IF YOU BELIEVE THE DEBT TO BE AN ERROR OR INVALID

Debt Collector: "Hello, can I speak to Charlie/is this Charlie?"

Charlie: "Who am I speaking with please?"

NOTE: At this stage, the law states that the debt collector must identify himself or herself as a debt collection agent

Debt Collector: "My name is Alex, a debt collector/collector from Dash Collections, the Collection agency representing Cups and Spoons Limited on your outstanding balance of $2,500. I need to know if you are ready to take care of the past due bill at this time."

Charlie: "Sir, I'm going to be recording this conversation, please kindly hold on while I turn on my recording device."

This is not only a time to turn on your recorder, turn it on but also take some time to ponder on the debt and try to remember if the statute of limitations on the debt has expired or otherwise—we talked about the statute of limitations earlier.

HOW TO DEAL WITH DEBT COLLECTORS

If you are unsure, return to the call.

Charlie: "Ask the following questions so that you can get it on record:

1. What is your name?
2. What is the name of the debt collection agency you represent?
3. What is the official address of the debt collection agency?
4. What is the name of the creditor?
5. How much does the creditor claim I owe?

Charlie: "I strongly believe I do not owe this particular debt. You can send me information on the debt according to the FDCPA so that I can review it. I am also revoking any permission you have to call me at any number so please make this your last call to me."

BE AWARE THAT:

Debt collectors also have their own script for communicating with debtors. Many of them are smart and will already anticipate these responses from smart debtors so they will try to ask some questions in a bid to extend the communication and make you say things you should not say.

They usually have 'baits' in their script and mostly, they will ignore your responses and stick to their own script. You should ignore these baits and avoid saying anything else to them after you have verbally disputed the debt and requested an official letter.

The only question you can answer after this is to verify your address. You should only verify or tell them *"Yes please"* or *"No, that is not my address."*

At no point should you give the debt collector your current address even if they get it wrong?

If the debt collector calls you back, turn on the recording device again and say something along the lines of, "I already disputed this debt and revoked permission for further calls the last time you called. Therefore, this call is in violation of the FDCPA rules and you leave me no choice but to report this violation to the relevant authorities"

Terminate the call after this and then wait for the letter giving more information about the debt. When you receive their letter, send them a 'debt dispute' letter along with a 'cease and desist' letter.

Later chapters will have samples of these letters.

How to Respond to Letters or Mails

A debt collector may choose to send you a letter instead of calling you. It is also important to know how to handle these types of correspondences the right way.

Here are a few guidelines to help you respond to debt collector's letters correctly:

Never Call Back

Sometimes, a debt collector will offer vague information in their letters to you and then urge you to call back so that they can now interrogate you and use their tactics on you in a phone conversation. You should avoid calling them altogether; you should only respond to them via letters or mail as well.

Never Provide any Information They Don't Already Have

If they do not have your address, do not give it to them. If they do not already have your phone number, do not give it to them. You should never give a debt collector any extra information about yourself, work, address, family, or anything else they do not already know.

Never Ignore Their Letters

Debt collection letters always come with a 30-day ultimatum after which the assumption is that you agree to the debt. It is important to reply to their letters as soon as you get it so that you can dispute the debt immediately.

Make sure you check the day of the letter postage to be sure that they left enough time to respond to the letter. If they only posted the letter 2 weeks before 30 days lapsed, then you can use that loophole against them in court.

Avoid Signing Documents from Debt Collection Agencies

Some debt collection agents will have no problem forging your signature on documents or tricking you to sign some documents. You should avoid signing documents from them. You can just write your name in full instead of signing documents.

Save Correspondences

Just as you would record conversations with debt collectors, you should save any copies of any letters you send to them or get from them.

HOW TO DEAL WITH DEBT COLLECTORS

HAVE THEM SIGN FOR LETTERS

Unscrupulous debt collectors can easily deny that they did not get your letters so make sure you use a reputable courier service that will have them sign for the letters so that you can keep evidence that they received your correspondences.

The procedure for dealing with debt collectors who send you letters is almost the same thing as dealing with those who choose to call you instead. You should immediately send them a letter to dispute the debt as well as a 'cease and desist' letter to stop them from contacting you about the debt.

If you do not owe the debt, know that the statute of limitation has passed, or do not wish to pay the debt, you should do the following:

- ❖ *First, you should send them a letter telling them to provide more information about the debt. Below a sample letter you can use below:*

SAMPLE LETTER ASKING FOR MORE INFORMATION FROM THE DEBT COLLECTOR

[Your Name]

[Your Address] *Use the same address they sent the initial letter to you

ERNIE BRAVEBOY

[Date]

[Collector's Name]

[Collector's Company Name and Address]

Subject: Re: The same subject the collector used or the account number of the debt

Dear (Collector)

I am writing to you regarding the letter you sent me (or the call you made to my phone) on (Date) about a debt that you are trying to collect.

You identified the debt as xxxxx amount owed to xxxxxx creditor for xxxxxx purpose.

To enable me to review the said debt, please kindly provide the following information:

1. The name and address of the creditor
2. The amount owed
3. The account number used by the creditor
4. The original creditor and account number of the creditor (if the debt started with a different creditor).
5. The amount owed to the original creditor and its transference date.
6. Any other name by which I may be able to identify the original creditor if they have another name apart from their official name.

HOW TO DEAL WITH DEBT COLLECTORS

7. Whom the current creditor obtained the debt from, and when they obtained it.

8. Documentation and verification or agreement made with the creditor that created a valid requirement for the debt repayment.

9. If someone else incurred the debt, and I am now being required to pay the debt, please kindly provide valid documentation and verification as to why I am required to pay the debt.

I also need you to provide details about the amount and age of the debt. Please kindly provide the following details:

1. A copy of the last billing statement that was sent to me by the original creditor.

2. All additional charges or interest fees (if any) from the last billing statement. This should include an itemized list showing the dates and the amounts added.

3. Documentation and verification that the agreement that created the debt also authorized the addition of the interest, fees, and charges.

4. The date the creditor claims the debt fell due when it subsequently became delinquent.

5. The date when the last payment was made on the particular account.

6. Any charges or deductions on this account including details about how they were calculated and documentation or authorization to make these

deductions or adjustments by the initial agreement that created the debt.

7. Evidence that the debt is actually within the statute of limitations

In addition to the above, I would like you to provide more details about the organization you represent before I can continue discussions about this debt with you. I will like to know:

1. If your debt collection agency is licensed to operate within xxxxx (your state) state
2. Name on the license, license number, and date
3. Name, address, and telephone number of the state that issued the license.

All of these will help me establish that you have the legal authority to collect this debt you claim I owe.

If you are licensed in a different state, please kindly provide evidence that your firm is licensed to operate in that state including details of the license issuing agency, name on the license, license number, and date, name, address and telephone number of the state that issued the license.

I need to hear from you as soon as possible to help me make an informed decision about this debt you claim I owe.

I am open to communicating with you about this matter; however in the meantime, please consider this debt as being in dispute and under discussion between us.

Thank you for your cooperation.

Kind regards,

[Your Name]

This letter requests information from debt collectors and on top to that, it helps scare scam or 'weak' debt collectors away because many of them usually do not have enough information or documentation to back up their claims.

Even the shrewdest of debt collectors is likely to turn 'jelly' after getting such a letter from a debtor because it means you know your rights, are ready to waste their time, not willing to pay, and cannot be intimidated.

- ❖ If after you receive the requested letter from the debt collector, you are sure it is an error or that you do not owe the said debt, send another letter telling them that you do not owe the debt along with a 'cease and desist' order to stop them from communicating with you.

Here is a sample letter to use:

SAMPLE DEBT DISPUTE WITH CEASE AND DESIST ORDER

[Your Name]

[Your Address] *Use the same address they sent the initial letter to you

[Date]

ERNIE BRAVEBOY

[Collector's Name]

[Collector's Company Name and Address]

Subject: Re: The same subject the collector used or the account number of the debt

Dear (Collector)

I am writing to you regarding the letter you sent me (or the call you made to my phone) on (Date) about a debt that you are trying to collect.

You identified the debt as xxxxx amount owed to xxxxxx creditor for xxxxxx purpose.

Having carefully reviewed the information you provided, I have concluded that I do not have any responsibility for the said debt.

Do not contact me about this debt anymore whether by phone, mail, letter, or any other platform or place.

If you decide to forward this debt to any other debt collection agency or report to any credit bureau or if you have already done so, I require you to report to them that this debt is disputed.

Thank you for your cooperation.

Yours sincerely,

[Your name]

HOW TO DEAL WITH DEBT COLLECTORS

❖ *If you do not wish to pay the debt or the statute of limitation has passed, send them a letter telling them to stop contacting you.*

ERNIE BRAVEBOY

Sample Cease and Desist Letter (If You Indeed Owe the Debt but Do Not Wish to Pay)

[Your Name]

[Your Address] *Use the same address they sent the initial letter to you

[Date]

[Collector's Name]

[Collector's Company Name and Address]

Subject: Re: The same subject the collector used or the account number of the debt

Dear (Collector)

I am writing to you regarding the letter you sent me (or the call you made to my phone) on (Date) about a debt that you are trying to collect.

You identified the debt as xxxxx amount owed to xxxxxx creditor for xxxxxx purpose.

Please cease all communication with me or this phone number/address about this debt.

Let it be on record that I dispute this debt and if you decide to report or have already reported this debt to any credit bureau, I require you to also report that this debt is disputed.

Thank you for your cooperation.

HOW TO DEAL WITH DEBT COLLECTORS

Yours sincerely,

[Your name]

- ❖ *If you have a lawyer and want them to deal with your lawyer instead (although the whole point of this book is so you can handle debt collectors yourself and save yourself some attorney fees), below is a sample letter to send:*

ERNIE BRAVEBOY

SAMPLE LETTER DIRECTING A DEBT COLLECTOR TO CONTINUE COMMUNICATIONS WITH YOUR LAWYER

[Your Name]

[Your Address] *Use the same address they sent the initial letter to you

[Date]

[Collector's Name]

[Collector's Company Name and Address]

Subject: Re: The same subject the collector used or the account number of the debt

Dear (Collector)

I am writing to you regarding the letter you sent me (or the call you made to my phone) on (Date) about a debt that you are trying to collect.

You identified the debt as xxxxx amount owed to xxxxxx creditor for xxxxxx purpose.

Please do not contact me directly about this debt anymore. Direct all communications to my lawyer.

My lawyer's contact information is:

[Contact Information]

Thank you for your cooperation.

Yours sincerely,

[Your name]

WHAT TO DO AFTER A DEBT COLLECTOR CONTACTS YOU

After a debt collector calls/sends you a letter with further information about the said debt, it is important for you to take some steps so that in the event that the debt collector decides to take legal actions against you, you can have an advantage over them.

Here is what you should do:

INVESTIGATE THE DEBT

Many debt collectors use fraudulent tactics: they try to intimidate you to pay money you do not owe and sometimes, the debt may be a case of identity theft, clerical errors, or any other errors. You should be sure what the case really is especially if you do not remember owing the debt the debt collector claims you owe.

Before you send your debt dispute letter, you should investigate the debt to be sure about what is really going on so that if the debt is an error, you can work on getting it removed from your credit report.

HOW TO INVESTIGATE A DEBT

To investigate the debt, you would have to:

ORDER YOUR CREDIT REPORT

We have three major credit-reporting bureaus; you are entitled to at least 2 copies of your credit report from these agencies yearly.

When you get notified about a debt especially one that you cannot remember or recognize, you should order your credit report and use it to trace the debt to see if you indeed owe what they claim you owe.

To get copies of your credit report, visit www.annualcreditreport.com.

How to Deal with Debt Collectors

Check Statute of Limitation

Next, you should confirm that the statute of limitation for the said debt has not passed. Check the date when the debt became delinquent, and find out what the statute of limitation for that type of debt is in your state to see if it has passed or not.

Reach out to the Creditor to Confirm

If you cannot find the said debt on your credit report and cannot remember the debt, there is a good chance that the debt collector is a fraud. Send a letter to the alleged creditor and request extensive information about the debts including when and how they were incurred, and the signed agreement between you and them. If the creditor fails to respond, you can cite this in court.

Dispute Errors in Your Credit Report

You have the right to dispute any errors on your credit report by contacting the credit bureau or hiring the services of a credit repair agency to help you remove the negative error from your credit report.

What You Should Never Do When Debt Collectors Contact You

Now you already know what to do when a debt collector contacts you. There are also a few things you should avoid doing.

Many people, out of panic perhaps, take some steps that end up hurting their cases in court because they already did some things that looked like an admission of guilt.

When a debt collector contacts you about a debt, you should never:

Try to Hide Your Money or Assets

Do not try to hide your money or assets even if a debt collector threatens to garnish your bank account or assets. The law considers it illegal and fraudulent to hide your assets especially when you indeed owe the debt.

Apply for a New Line of Credit

The law also considers it fraudulent to abandon an old account and apply for a new line of credit when you are unable to pay what you owe other creditors.

Negotiate with Them Before Debt Validation

HOW TO DEAL WITH DEBT COLLECTORS

When a debt collector calls you about a debt, they do not expect you to know so much about the legal process and they are not expecting you to ask for debt validation documents; they will, therefore, try to get you to negotiate a settlement with them. Do not fall for this trap. If you want to negotiate, make sure you negotiate after you receive the debt validation documents.

STEPS TO TAKE IF A DEBT IS TRUE AND VALID

If you indeed owe the debt and the statute of limitation is yet to pass, then there are two options to take:

1: NEGOTIATE AN OFFER TO PAY A PALTRY SUM

If you do not like the idea of being taken to court or reported to credit bureaus, then you can try to negotiate a settlement with the agency.

The truth is that debt collectors are willing to accept anything you offer them because they bought the debts from the original creditors for next to nothing so anything you offer them is still a profit for them. However, do not expect them to give in easily. Many of them will want to act tough and reject your offer.

If you use the tips I am about to give you, you will be able to negotiate with them successfully, and pay whatever you can afford.

HOW TO NEGOTIATE WITH DEBT COLLECTORS

You should:

Step 1: Decide How Much You Wish to Pay

You should offer to pay between 10-15% of the amount you owe and no more than that. Usually, they will try to get you to increase your offer; simply tell them that you cannot afford anything above that. They may also try to ask you questions about your assets, wages, and other personal questions. You do not have to answer any of these questions.

Step 2: Record the Negotiation Process

Debt collectors may negotiate with you and then after you have paid, they may do a double take and start claiming you negotiated with the wrong person and the person did not have the authority to make such decisions. All of this is in a bid to get you to part with some more money. Make sure you record the conversations (if your state allows it) or communicate via mail alone so that you can keep a record of the negotiation process.

Step 3: Negotiate a Full and Final Settlement

Make sure you always use the word "full and final settlement" when you are negotiating with debt collectors. Debt collectors are always fishing and looking for loopholes and therefore, when you negotiate with them and pay them off, they may come after you again claiming the money you paid was not in full and final settlement, and instead, was a part-payment and you still owe them.

When this happens, it becomes more difficult to win against them in court because making one payment means you already accept that you owe the debt and therefore, the law expects you to repay the debt.

Step 4: Ask for, and Sign a Debt Settlement Agreement Before You Make Payments

After negotiating with the debt collector, make sure you sign a debt settlement agreement with the debt collection agency before you make any payments so that they cannot come after you again in the future, and they cannot sell the debt to anyone else: they have to close the case after payment.

Step 5: Ask the Negative Report to be removed from Your Credit Report

If the debt has already been reported to a credit bureau, you must also negotiate with the debt collection agency to have the negative report removed from your credit report as one of the conditions for settlement.

Make sure this is also included in the debt settlement agreement you will co-sign with the debt collection agency. You should only make payments after the fulfillment of these conditions.

2: Call Their Bluff and See What Happens Next

If you call a collector's bluff by sending your cease and desist letter, the debt collector may decide to let you off the hook especially if what you owe is not worth going to court over.

However, the debt collector may decide to take any two courses of action:

1. Take you to court
2. Report to Credit Bureaus

HOW TO DEAL WITH DEBT COLLECTORS

The next chapter discusses how to handle the situation if the debt collector decides to take you to court.

Chapter 4: How to Beat a Debt Collection Agent in Court

One cool day, when sited at home or at work, you suddenly receive a certified letter from a law firm informing you that a debt collection agency is suing you for a debt you allegedly owe. It is normal to feel scared, feel bad, or have any other strong emotions about this situation because really, no one likes to have a court case.

There is no need to panic or let the situation intimidate you because this is what the debt collectors want: they want you to go into panic mode and probably call them up for a chance to settle the case out of court.

There is no need to do this either because as you are about to discover, there are numerous ways to outfox debt collectors and win against them in court after they sue you.

Follow the steps laid out in this chapter and there is a great chance that you will be able to win a debt collection case.

Step 1: Reply to the Summons

Many people choose to ignore the summons; this is wrong. As soon as you receive the letter, read it and look for important information within the letter.

Make sure you confirm that the letter is a genuine one since many desperate debt collectors often forge court summons. Confirm that the letter is an original.

Next, look at how many days you have to respond to the letter and state your readiness to defend yourself in court.

Reply to the letter stating your willingness to defend yourself immediately so that a date can be set for a hearing.

Please take note of that date and make sure you are in court on that day. If you do not show up, you lose the case by default and the court shall rule in favor of the collection company. This means you will now be compelled to pay the debt and the debt collector can garnish your wages or other allowable assets.

Step 2: Decide if You Need a Lawyer or Not

If the debt collector filed the case in a magisterial court, you can easily defend yourself using the defenses laid out later in this chapter. For higher courts though, you will need the services of a lawyer to defend you in court. However, you do not have to hire an expensive lawyer. You can hire an affordable one, prepare your defense using the tips in this book, and then hand it over to the lawyer.

Step 3: File a Request for Production

After responding to the summons, the next thing you need to do is to file a document called a "request for production."

This document is sent to the lawyer of the debt collection company and is simply a request that they provide you with a copy of the original agreement you made with the creditor with your signature on it.

The truth is that many debt collectors will not be able to produce this document because many creditors, utility companies, and credit card companies are bad record keepers.

Even when they have these records, it is sometimes very difficult for creditors to find these documents and give them to the debt collection company because it simply means that they will have to sift through thousands of documents to find this agreement.

The moment a creditor sells a debt to a debt buyer for a few pennies, they are done with that debt. They do not want their business activities disrupted by it so except in cases where the creditor operates a computerized file keeping system where it becomes easy to just pull out the records and give it to the debt collector to help their case, there is a significant chance that the debt collector will be unable to produce this document.

You file a request for production of the original contract you signed with the creditor by sending a letter that looks like this to the lawyer of the debt collector.

[Your Name]

[Your Address]

[The Name of the Court]

HOW TO DEAL WITH DEBT COLLECTORS

[The Name of the Original Creditor] }   Docket Number: [Insert]

[Plaintiff]   }   REQUEST FOR PRODUCTION

Versus   }

  [Your Name]   }

  [Defendant]   }

The Defendant requests that the Plaintiff [Name of Original Creditor] produce the following documents in connection with this matter. In the event that objection is made, please state the reason for the objection. If denying the matter, please provide details about the reason why the answering party cannot provide the requested documents.

Please provide:

1. A copy of the application for credit signed by the defendant.

2. A copy of the initial executed contract in [name of original creditor]'s possession setting forth the terms that the defendant allegedly agreed to in connection with the credit.

3. If any modifications were made to the initial contract, kindly provide a copy of modification agreement allegedly signed by the defendant.

4. A copy of all statements, invoices, or receipts on the account from the inception till date.

5. Details regarding the alleged charges including how they were charged, reasons for the charges, amount charged and the dates the charges were made.

6. Evidence of all payments received by the creditor on the account from the inception till date.

[Print date]

[Your Name]

[Your Signature]

CC: [Name of the Judge]

[Name of the Lawyer Representing the Creditor]

After writing this letter, print it, send a copy to the judge and another copy to the lawyer, and wait to see what happens.

What this letter does is warn the lawyer of the debt collection company that you are aware of your rights, that they do not have legal rights to the money they are trying to collect, and that you will be ready to go toe to toe with them in court.

Many debt collectors will drop the case at this point because they know that they do not have these documents. However, some will still like to proceed to court.

STEP 4: PREPARE YOUR DEFENSE

Preparing your defense is all about looking for loopholes in the debt collector's case and methods that you can legally exploit to let yourself off the hook.

Here are a few defenses you can use against debt collectors in the court of law:

The Attachment Rule

In most states, the law requires that debt collectors or debt buyers must attach a copy of the written contract between the original creditor and debtor.

If the debt collector did not attach the document in their correspondences to you or in the letter sent you to inform you that they are suing you, you can file a motion in court requesting that they produce the document or that the case be dismissed if they cannot produce it.

Debt Limits for Law Suits

Find out what the minimum amount collectors are legally allowed to sue for in small claims courts within your state. Many states have limits for this and you can petition the court to dismiss the case if the amount you are being sued for does not fall within the limit.

Debt Validation

When the debt collector initially contacted you to inform you about the debt and you requested for more information about the debt, did they send it to you within the 5 days specified by the FDCPA law? If they did not, you can exploit this error and use against the debt collector in court.

"Accord and Satisfaction"

Another thing you can use in your defense is the debt satisfaction rule called "Accord and satisfaction."

Many utility companies and credit card companies usually take up insurance policies to protect their businesses from defaulters. If the original creditor has taken any compensation from insurance companies or has had a tax deduction for the loss their businesses incurred from the bad debt, then the loss is regarded as satisfied and the debt collector is not legally allowed to take you to court for a debt that has been satisfied.

HOW TO DEAL WITH DEBT COLLECTORS

Statute of Limitation

Find out what the statute of limitation for that type of debt is in your state. Be sure that the statute of limitation has not passed and if it has, you can bring this to the notice of the court and ask for a dismissal of the case.

"Scienti et Violenti nonfit Injuria"

In English, this translates to "An injury is not done to one who knows and wills it.

What this implies is that under the law, a person cannot make claims for damages or sue another person for it if they willingly and knowingly put themselves in harm's way.

Debt collectors are often aware that the debts they are inheriting are bad and delinquent debts, yet they go ahead to buy those debts thereby willfully putting themselves in harm's way.

You can cite this in court and ask the court to dismiss the case.

Statute of Frauds

A debt collection agent that is unable to produce an agreement you made with them (not the creditor this time) yet claim that you owe them, may be petitioned under the statute of fraud.

You entered into an agreement with the credit card company, utility company or whoever the creditor; you did not enter into an agreement with the collection agency and they did not provide any services to you and therefore, for them to claim that you owe them is fraudulent.

You can cite the statute of frauds in court to get the case dismissed.

Lack of Privity

A similar defense you can cite in court is "Lack of privity."

What this means is that when you were entering into a contract with the creditor, you did not enter into a contract with the debt collector. Therefore, and according to the Fair Debt Collection Practices Act that states that:

"The debt collector cannot collect any amount of money that is not authorized by the agreement creating the debt or permitted by the law because there is no agreement between the collector and the alleged debtor, no collection can be sustained",

...no relationship exists between the plaintiff and the defendant, and the debt collection agency cannot collect any money not permitted or authorized by the agreement.

Meeting of the Minds

For a contract to be considered legally valid, there has to be something called "meeting of the minds".

Meeting of the minds represents a mutual agreement and a common understanding between the parties to the contract. The debt collection agency was not a party to the contract and there is no document to support the claims by the debt collector that there was a party to the contract between you and the original creditor at the inception when the contract was originally created. Therefore, no contract exists between the debt collection agency and the defendant, and you are under no obligation to pay them any money.

Failure of Consideration

If the debt collection agency is claiming that there is a valid contract with them, then where is the consideration? For a contract to be valid, there has to be something legally referred to as consideration.

Consideration means there must be an exchange of benefits between the parties entering into the contract. Since there was no exchange of goods or money between you and the debt collection agency, there is no consideration and therefore, no binding contract between you and the debt collection agency. In other words, you do not owe them any money.

Insufficient Specifity in the Pleading

In simple terms, this means that the debt collector must provide specific details about how the debts came to be. They need to specify:

1. What Goods or Services led to the debt?

2. How much and how frequently were the purchases or charges made to the debtor's account.

You can cite the debt collection law that states that:

> "A defendant is entitled to know the dates on which individual transactions were made, the amounts, and the items purchased to be able to answer intelligently and determine what items he can admit and what items he can contest" Marine Bank, 25 pa. D. 7 C 3d at 267-69."

If the debt collector cannot provide sufficient information about the purchases made or services allegedly enjoyed, then they do not have enough facts about the debt to be able to come after you from a legal standpoint.

HOW TO START YOUR DEFENSE IN COURT

On the day of the hearing, the first thing you should say in court is:

> "Defendant is without information or sufficient knowledge to form an opinion as to the truth or accuracy of Plaintiff's claim, and based on that, denies generally and specifically the Plaintiff's claim."

HOW TO DEAL WITH DEBT COLLECTORS

Here, you are referring to the fact that the debt collector has failed to provide all the documents you requested for and therefore, it is impossible for you to know if you actually owe the debt that they claim you do or not.

This is the first statement you should read out in court. After this, it is possible that the debt collector's lawyer will call you to the stands, place you under oath and then brandish some papers in your face asking if you deny signing 'this contract'.

Usually, what the lawyer is trying to do here is to trick you to admit to signing a contract with the creditor or debt collection agent since you are under oath and know the implication of lying under oath. However, and is usually the case, what the lawyer will be flashing before you is not the contract you signed but a decoy, an empty piece of paper because they usually do not have copies of the original contract from the creditor.

Regardless of what the debt collector's lawyer says, whether they indeed have the contract or not, as long as they did not send it to you at any point before the hearing date, just continue to stick to this statement

"Defendant is without information or sufficient knowledge to form an opinion.........................."

Continue to repeat this no matter what the lawyer asks you about the contract or signed contract, the judge will lose his or her patience eventually and order the plaintiff to move on to other questions or sit down after which you may now move on to the other defenses discussed in this chapter.

Pick each one, read it to the judge, and remember to be confident and stick to your script no matter the level of intimidation or tricks used by the debt collector's lawyers.

I am certain that, using what you have learned in this guide, you shall be able to get yourself off the debt collector's hook without many hassles or spending too much. However, if you are not confident enough to defend yourself in court, consider hiring a lawyer and discussing these defenses with your lawyer so that he or she can know which loopholes to exploit to be able to get you off the hook.

Conclusion

We have come to the end of the book. Thank you for reading and congratulations on reading until the end.

With all the tips and guidelines laid out in this book, I have no doubt that you will be able to beat any debt collection agent at their game whether they decide to take you to court or not.

If the collection agency decides to report you to credit bureaus and hurt your credit score instead of taking you to court, you can take some steps to have your credit report repaired.

You can refer to my other book in the series to learn how to repair your credit.

If you found the book valuable, can you recommend it to others? One way to do that is to post a review on Amazon.

Please leave a review for this book on Amazon!

Thank you and good luck!

CREDIT REPAIR

How to Repair Your Credit All by Yourself

A Beginners Guide to Better Credit

ERNIE BRAVEBOY

INTRODUCTION

I want to thank you and congratulate you for buying the book, "Credit Repair: How to Repair Your Credit All by Yourself - A Beginners Guide to Better Credit".

Discovering that you have poor credit comes at the most inopportune of moments. Most people only find out that their credit score is bad when trying to borrow money from the bank for, say, a mortgage. Poor credit makes it very hard for the bank, or any lender for that matter, to loan you money, and even when they do, the interest rates attached are often absurdly high: it often feels as if they are trying to punish you.

As such, it is vital that you be aware of the state of your credit. If it is, as they say, "in a bad way," the thing to do is to face the problem and set out to try to fix it. Otherwise, it will come back to haunt you and you best believe it: bad credit always comes back to haunt.

This book will give you the bulk of information, tools, and knowledge you need to embark on an intensive credit repair process that will help you build a positive credit score.

Thanks again for buying this book. I hope you enjoy it!

ERNIE BRAVEBOY

© Copyright 2018 by Ernie Braveboy
All rights reserved.

This document is geared towards providing exact and reliable information in regards to the topic and issue covered. The publication is sold with the idea that the publisher is not required to render an accounting, officially permitted, or otherwise, qualified services. If advice is necessary, legal or professional, a practiced individual in the profession should be ordered.

- From a Declaration of Principles which was accepted and approved equally by a Committee of the American Bar Association and a Committee of Publishers and Associations.

In no way is it legal to reproduce, duplicate, or transmit any part of this document by either electronic means or in printed format. Recording of this publication is strictly prohibited and any storage of this document is not allowed unless with written permission from the publisher. All rights reserved.

The information provided herein is stated to be truthful and consistent, in that any liability, in terms of inattention or otherwise, by any usage or abuse of any policies, processes, or directions contained within is the solitary and utter responsibility of the recipient reader. Under no circumstances will any legal responsibility or blame be held against the publisher for any reparation, damages, or monetary loss due to the information herein, either directly or indirectly.

Respective authors own all copyrights not held by the publisher.

The information herein is offered for informational purposes solely and is universal as so. The presentation of the information is without a contract or any type of guarantee assurance.

The trademarks that are used are without any consent, and the publication of the trademark is without permission or backing by the trademark owner. All trademarks and brands within this book are for clarifying purposes only and are the owned by the owners themselves, not affiliated with this document.

SECTION 1: UNDERSTANDING CREDIT & CREDIT SCORE

Chapter 1: Understanding Your Credit Score

This chapter does not intend to analyze your particular score and give you several dozen reasons why it is what it is. This will come later and even then, we will keep it non-sensationalistic. This chapter aims to explain what credit score is; it also aims to show you what goes into a credit score.

What Is Your Credit Score?

As you may already know, your credit score is a 3-digit number generated from information that appears in your credit score, by a mathematical algorithm. Above all other things, a credit score is, by design, supposed to "predict risk."

You see, the bank or lender has no way of truly knowing if a borrower is honest and prompt in repaying back loaned amounts except by going by his or her credit score. Your credit score shows the bank or any other lender just how high the probability of not honoring credit obligations is, in the 24 months or so after the generation of your score. Going by this, it is clear that the primary use of the credit score is to "define you" to the bank or lender.

As far as the credit score goes, there are multiple scoring models available. Of them all, the FICO credit score is the dominant model. Whether you choose to take them at their word or not, www.myFICO.com claim that well over 90% of all US institutions employ FICO scores as they try and make financial decisions.

What Is The FICO Score Range?

The FICO score ranges from 300 to 850, with 300 being the base score and 850 being the highest possible score. A higher number is indicative of lower risk.

As a consumer, you will have 3 FICO scores. Each FICO score will come in each of the three credit reports that you have a right to. The three major bureaus: Transunion, Experian, and Equifax provide these credit reports.

NOTE: Unfortunately, today, you can only access FICO scores on both Equifax and Transunion. Experian ended its agreement with FICO in 2009. However, other credit score models will be included in the Experian report).

What Goes Into Your Credit Score?

The data from the credit report will go into five major categories that will make up the FICO score. Naturally, the model will consider some factors more significant, factors such as a debt owed and payment history. Here are the categories:☐

1: Payment History (35%)

This shows payment information on your account.

2: Amounts Owed (30%)

This points to how much you owe. The credit amount available and in use is heavily weighted.

3: LENGTH OF CREDIT HISTORY (15%)

This points to how long ago you opened your accounts as well as time since account activity.

4: CREDIT TYPE USED (10%)

This is the "accounts mix" you have. There are varied account types such as installment and revolving.

5: NEW CREDIT (10%)

This is the pursuit of new credit. This is inclusive of credit inquiries as well as the total number of newly opened accounts.

NOTE: Chapter 4 will have a proper evaluation of each of these five categories.

Chapter 2: Understanding Credit Reports

What is a credit report and how often should you expect one? What can you expect to see your credit reports?

In the most simplistic of terms, a credit report is a "compilation of information" regarding the way you go about handling debt. It includes information on how much debt you have managed to accrue, how you go about paying your bills (are you always on time or behind?), where you work, where you go home to, if you have ever filed for bankruptcy, and whether your vehicle has ever been repossessed or your house foreclosed.

Does it look as though the credit report has too much information? Well, if it looks that way, it is because it actually does.

How Does Information Get On The Credit Report?

TIP: Credit bureaus are the ones that (usually) maintain credit reports. Credit bureaus, or credit reporting agencies, are businesses that specialize in credit management.

The previous chapter mentioned the three major credit bureaus in the US: <u>Equifax</u>, <u>Experian</u>, and <u>Transunion</u>. Corporations that do business with you have an agreement with the credit bureaus to send information to them (or at the very least, to send information to one of them.) These bureaus will then update the information they receive on your credit report. Most of your loan accounts and credit cards are updated on the credit report on a monthly basis.

Regarding the last sentence of the previous paragraph, this is not always the case with all businesses. Not all businesses will update the bureaus on your financial information on a monthly basis. However, the bulk of these businesses will indeed get in touch with the bureaus once you do not make your payments.

Here is an example: your cable bill will usually not be included in your credit report. However, if you do fall 6 months behind in payments, you can expect the cable company to tell on you, and the cable bill to appear on your credit report.

What Type of Information Is Included In The Credit Report?

This is a mere overview to help you understand what your credit report really is; a more detailed evaluation of this will be available in the next chapter.

A credit report is a lot like an over glorified identity card in that it contains your basic identity information: your name, home address, place of employment, etc.

You must understand that your credit report may not always be perfect. There may be mistakes such as misspellings of your name as well as inaccurate addresses and employers. At times, this is because of mistakes made by the business that forwarded your information. At other times, this may be because of identity theft.

As such, it is very important that you go through all your credit reports with a fine toothcomb. It could be that your credit is suffering through no fault of your own, and you are atoning for someone else's financial sins.

Checking Your Credit Report

It is important that you order your credit report at least once a year as a way to ensure that the information on it is correct. If you are trying to repair your credit, it is wise to order it with more frequency. The same applies to a case where you are gearing to apply for a major loan. If you suspect you are a victim of identity theft, insist on frequent credit reports and then report any mishaps that recur to these bureaus.

NOTE: You have a right to one free credit report from all three credit bureaus every year. Chapter 6 also shows you how you can access these credit reports.

What Can You Expect To See On Your Credit Report?

As this very chapter has indicated, a credit report will have basic personal details such as your name, your date of birth, your address, and the likes. As we said in an earlier part of this chapter, it is of utmost importance that you perform a thorough evaluation of the information contained in your credit report to ensure it is accurate. Note, however, that past addresses appearing on your credit report are not a bad thing. Here are other elements you can expect to see on your credit report:

1. Your credit report will also list any financial issues of the legal kind that you may have had. Here, we are talking the likes of liens, wage garnishment, judgment, and bankruptcy. If you have any of these elements on your credit score, understand that they may be a major reason why your credit score is so poor. However, take comfort in the fact that these elements will not dictate the state of your credit forever; they should not have to anyway. At the very least, even if you are passive in trying to repair them, they will inevitably age off.

2. Your credit report will also contain creditor information. In fact, this is what will make up the bulk of your credit report. This is inclusive of different accounts that you have (think credit cards, loans, and the like), their present status (closed, opened, in collections, etc.), credit limits, balances, as well as details on payment frequency. Of course, if you have some missed payments, you can mostly expect them to show up and to contribute to the overall weight of your score. The same applies for late payments. It is from all these details that your credit score is generated.

I believe that you now understand what makes up your credit report as well as your credit score. The next logical step is to understand what makes an excellent or poor credit score.

The next chapter covers this in detail.

Chapter 3: What Makes a Credit Score Excellent or Poor

Your credit score is somewhat like a disciplinary record as far as finance and credit management goes. The lower your credit score, the more likely it is that you are not great at managing your finances and as such, you are an unnecessary risk, at least as far as getting a loan goes.

A person with a high credit score, on the other hand, is an attractive individual to banks and lenders: he or she can ask for any amount desired, and the bank or lender is likely to give it whilst keeping interest rates favorable (usually).

Think about it this way: a fellow with a high credit score could decide to take up a loan tomorrow, be it to finance a new car or a new house, and he or she would be confident of getting it. To them, it is a matter of WHEN they can access the loan. If you, on the other hand, have a less than desirable credit score, it really is a matter of IF you can get the loan. As such, your credit score is something you should take very seriously.

This chapter will revisit the factors introduced in Chapter 1 and add flesh to them for they are the factors that carry all the weight with regard to the state of your credit score.

Factor #1: Payment History

This will account for the biggest slice of your credit score. Just how well do you pay off your bills every month? Given that a whopping 35% of the credit score relies on this one, it may be time to take monthly bills more seriously.

Under every loan you have ever taken, under every credit card or mortgage you have ever had, you will be able to see on your credit report, how much money you have paid towards it for a stretch of time, in comparison to the total monthly period of the particular loan. If the monthly bill totals $551 and you barely ever pay over $300 towards this bill in a month, this will tell a story that will be all too apparent, going by your credit score.

Other creditors will rarely bother to update the bureaus monthly but will do so once the payments fall behind by several months. Such companies include utility companies, cell phone companies, and cable services.

If there are late payments on the credit report, there will be information on just how late these payments were. The later the payment is, the more you can expect the credit score to fall.

Factor #2: Your Total Debt

30% of your FICO score will be relative to how much debt you have accrued. Installment loans such as student loans and mortgages will not weigh quite as heavily as, for example, your revolving debt.

Your revolving debt is inclusive of your credit cards. Lenders tend to keep a keen eye on your debt-to-credit ratio. They like to call it "credit utilization." Your debt-to-credit-ratio, or credit utilization, calculate just how much you owe in comparison to the maximum credit line present in your credit cards.

If you are close to maxing out a card you own, you can bet that your credit score suffers as a result. Here is the thing, however—we are speaking ratios here. Two fellows can owe the same debt on their card but end up having a very wide difference, with regard to their credit scores, if their maximum balances differ.

Here is an example:

A person with $3,000 debt on his credit card, with a $10,000 maximum balance only has 30% credit utilization. Another person with a similar $3,000 credit card charged amount but with a halved credit card limit of $5,000 is walking around with a 60% ratio. Assuming all other things are equal, the $5,000 credit limit fellow will have a much lower score.

FACTOR #3: CREDIT HISTORY LENGTH

This will account for 15% of your credit score. This is because a lender cannot possibly gauge your willingness, or ability, to repay loans if you do not have some sort of record proving that you can be able to do so. The scoring model will take into account just how long various accounts you own have been open, inclusive of credit cards and loans.

Here is some mood-dampening news. Rent payments are never part of the FICO score (If they were, the absolute top tip, with regard to repairing your credit, would have a lot to do with having your rental payments reflect on your credit report. But then again, your credit would likely not be bad.)

Factor #4: New Credit

When you read your credit report, you will see a section called "inquiries." "Inquiries" simply refers to every credit application you have submitted over the last 24 months. This can affect up to 10% of your overall score.

Each inquiry present will take off 5 or so points from your score during the 1st year. The exception will be if you completed multiple inquiries within a few weeks. If this is your situation, then it is merely indicative that you went out for some rate shopping for a credit card or loan. That batch of inquiries, thus, will be treated as just one inquiry.

Factor #5: Credit Mix

This will contribute to the final 10% of your score. The types of credit you have will contribute to how high your score is. In this very chapter, we mention that revolving debt, inclusive of credit cards, will heavily influence your credit score when compared to installment loans. Installment loans will usually have some asset or other tied to them, such as a car or a house.

One major reason why installment loans will have less of a negative influence on your credit score is that they signal that you have some asset of value that you are naturally committed to paying for, so you can continue to own it. It is very hard to say the same for purchases you make on impulse, on your credit card, which is why the penalty is higher for these.

Student loans have a favorable outlook primarily because they signal an investment into future earning power. In truth, the lender is a very simple entity, with a proclivity toward thinking linearly. The lender will say, *"If this guy took out this student loan to pay for his law degree, then he will be able to make more money in a few years. The more money this guy makes, the faster he will be able to pay off his loans. Even more importantly, the more money this guy makes, the more he will be able to put himself in a position to borrow more from us, which means more profits."*

If you can monitor and manage these factors well, you can build a positive credit score even if yours is in bad shape right now. Later chapters of this guide will show you how to repair a bad credit score.

In the next chapter, we will discuss why you should repair your credit score (in other words, the implications of having a bad credit score)

Chapter 4: Why Repair Poor Credit

You probably have more than a few ideas why it is important to repair poor credit. Regardless, this chapter is a necessary read all the same.

There are so many reasons why it is necessary to maintain a healthy credit score—that is beside the obvious one of being able to walk to the bank and being eligible for a loan.

Let us examine some reasons why you must maintain healthy credit.

#1: You Save A Lot of Money on Interest

You already know this one, but here it is anyway: *a low credit score only prompts the lender to raise the interest charged.*

The lower your credit score, the higher you can expect the interest charged on loans to be, and this is if you are lucky enough to convince the lender that you are a worthy prospect of a loan.

Once you repair your credit, you will immediately enjoy competitive interest rates. Do you know why lenders will suggest absurdly high-interest rates and believe they can get away with it? Because not only does your poor credit show that you are untrustworthy, the lender knows that your lending options are severely limited because of your less than desirable credit.

#2: You Will Not Have To Pay High-Security Deposits

Utility service companies—even phone companies—like to check a person's credit score before allowing the said person to establish service. If the score is poor, these service providers charge a deposit to, in their words, "offset the risk of default." Only when you make your payments on time will you be able to get back your deposit. ☐

#3: You Will Be Able To Get A Lower Insurance Rate

This is not something we made up for this book: the state of your credit determines your insurance premiums. This includes all sorts of insurances: life, auto, home, and the likes. Simply put, a bad credit history will mean paying more for insurance than you otherwise would with healthy credit in place.

#4: You Will Not Be Compelled To Pay With Cash For Just About Everything

Bad credit makes it difficult to get credit cards. This will mean having to walk around with cash everywhere. This will likely not be something that puts you off... until you need to do something like rent a car. Renting a car will require you to pay an extra deposit amount if you do not pay using a credit card.

#5: You Will Be Eligible For A Higher Credit Limit

HOW TO REPAIR YOUR CREDIT ALL BY YOURSELF

Once you show that you can pay your bills on time—the creditor will be very eager to increase your credit limit. However, your creditor will still check your credit score just to be sure that you are truly deserving of an increased credit limit. Here is when things start to get interesting: if your credit score is outright poor, the creditor may actually decide that, rather than being deserving of a credit limit increase, your credit limit actually needs slashing.

SECTION 2: NEGATIVE ITEMS ON THE CREDIT REPORT

Chapter 5: Evaluating Negative Items That May Appear On Your Credit Report

Before we go on ahead and examine negative items on your credit report, here are a few things to understand:

1. The FCRA limits the time length that a credit bureau may report negative items on the credit report. The same bureau(s) will often report positive as well as neutral items indefinitely.

2. The extent to which every negative item hurts your credit score will fade gradually, albeit slowly, with time. The lesson here is that unless you go ahead and ignore this book's call to implement positive credit behavior, it is impossible to have bad credit forever.

3. Negative items do not have to sit and stew for years until time peels them off. It is very possible to remove negative items from your credit report much earlier than their expiry date. However, this is not always possible and always depends on your unique situation, and if your request to have them taken off is acceptable to the creditor. Still, if you write to the bureaus and ask nicely, the probability of them taking the blemish off your credit report tends to be high, especially since so very few people bother to write and ask. But then again, not many

people go out of their way to read positive, actionable credit repair material as you are doing right now.

4. The smart man or woman is far more aggressive with the removal of more recent negative items than with the older ones. The logic behind this is simple enough: the older the negative item is, the sooner it will age out and fall off your annual credit report. Newer negative items will be around for long. Unless the older negative item is truly hurting any chances of getting a higher credit score, focus the bulk of your energy towards "prematurely" removing newer negative items.

With all of this said, let us look at the types of negative items you may find on your credit report. You will also discover how long you can expect these items to sit around if you do not go out of your way to have them removed early:

ITEM #1: CHARGE-OFFS

A charge off will occur when the creditor makes the decision that they may not be able to collect your debt. Instead of having the debt on their books and have it registered as debt that is past its due date, the creditor decides to eliminate the debt from past due accounts in their books.

It does not end there, however. By having the debt charged off, the company sees its accounts receivable report automatically improve. Still, this does not mean that the debt is cleared off and has disappeared. In a majority of cases, the debt will be sold to a debt buyer (yes, debt buyers exist), who will pay the company and then go right ahead and expect that you pay the full amount owed.

The debt buyer will insist that you pay the full amount owed, inclusive of the likes of court fees, late charges, interest, etc. The debt buyer will more or less make sure that they miss nothing.

You may be asking yourself what court fees have to do with any of this. Well, these debt buyers prefer to collect by contacting you and immediately taking you to court so they can collect the full value of the debt and applicable fees that arise. A charge off is not a desirable thing to have hanging over your credit.☐

A charge off can sit and stew on your credit report for up to 7 years and a further 180 days.

Item #2: Collections

Collections tend to be tricky things because paying them off could actually inflict more damage to your credit score as the starting date of when the collection was reported may be reset.

Never jump straight into paying off a collection: read all the paperwork available until you understand everything. Use the services of a lawyer if you have to, but make sure that you go through everything carefully and understand how every available course of action will affect your credit.

Just like a charge off and if unaddressed, a collection will hover for 7 years from the day that you first fell behind.

Item #3: Late Payments

It will not matter if you actually catch up on the amounts you owe. Any payment that you fall behind paying for 30 days can appear on your credit report. The positive news here is that many creditors tend to hold off reporting a late payment until you get too comfortable and have a 2nd late payment. You see, they do not want to upset good customers, also known as biting the hand that feeds them.

Lenders can report late payments for up to 7 years.

ITEM #4: BANKRUPTCIES

Bankruptcies will be reported for "no more than 10 years" from the filing date, which in itself, despite its sympathetic nature, is not a line that will make most people smile. 10 years is a long time to have your credit dragged down by a negative item. If your case is dismissed, then the countdown begins from the date of dismissal.

ITEM #5: FORECLOSURES

A foreclosure may be reported for up to 7 years. However, this one tends to be very easy to walk around. Once you get your financial balance back, you could always go on and buy a new house, as well as seek to have the foreclosure removed by writing to the bureaus.

ITEM #6: JUDGMENTS

These may appear for up to 7 years from the filing date of the lawsuit or until the governing limitations statute expires—whichever hangs around for longer. Most limitation statutes tend to expire sooner than 7 years, and as such, we are talking about 7 years as a maximum.

Item #7: Repossessions

These may be reported for up to 7 years.

Item #8: Tax Liens

The taxman is brutal here, seeing as, under federal law, tax liens that go unpaid may be reported indefinitely. However, credit bureaus often decide 10 years is long enough to have these appear and subsequently remove them after a decade.

Now that we have the basics out of the way, the chapters from this one onwards will show you how to overhaul your credit score. To do so, the first thing you need to do is give your credit report, once you have it, a thorough evaluation.

SECTION 3: OVERHAULING YOUR CREDIT STATE

Chapter 6: Step 1 – Thoroughly Evaluate Each Credit Report

Well, we are somewhat putting the cart before the horse here. Before making a thorough evaluation of the credit reports, naturally, the first thing you need to do is to access them.

As this book has said, there are 3 credit bureaus—Experian, Transunion, and Equifax—and you have a right to at least one credit report from each of these bureaus yearly.

Assuming you have not accessed your credit reports or you have had some trouble trying to access them, here is how you can access your free report:

1. Go to www.AnnualCreditReport.com

2. The interface is simple and direct: enter the personal information requested. You will have to answer a few security-related questions, which is necessary because it guards against malicious identity thieves.

3. After verifying your identity, the portal will redirect you to a page where you will be able to download all credit reports from the 3 bureaus. It should not take too long to download them—unless you have a slow internet connection.

4. If you are an old-fashioned person who likes to have hardcopy versions along with the softcopy ones, you can

call 1-877-322-8228, verify your identity to the consumer care personality at the end of the line, and request hard copies of your credit reports mailed to your address.

With this out of the way, let us look at thoroughly evaluating each credit report:

THOROUGHLY EVALUATING EACH CREDIT REPORT: HOW TO

Once you have accessed your credit reports, the next logical step is to go over them with a fine toothcomb and check them for accuracy. The 3 credit reports will not necessarily be the same because some creditors only bother to report to one or two of the three bureaus. Thus, having one item appearing in one or two reports, but missing from the third one, does not outright mean reporting mistakes.

Still, you should carefully check and determine the accuracy of the reporting. A creditor may only report to two out of three bureaus, but the information appears differently on both reports. The creditor could report to all 3 bureaus but the information is only similar in two out of the three credit reports.

Never assume that the information is similar across all 3 reports. Check to make sure it is.

Here is a simplistic guide on how to evaluate your credit reports thoroughly:

1. The first step is to make sure that basic personal information is recorded correctly. Ensure that there are

HOW TO REPAIR YOUR CREDIT ALL BY YOURSELF

no other persons listed on your credit report. Only after doing this should you proceed to the rest of the points here.

2. Take note of any section that appears incorrectly reported, from the account opening date to highest balance had. Be especially thorough on negative items, such as reported late payments. Make sure that you indeed own all credit lines.

3. Focus more on the report's negative report section and ensure everything is accurate. You will find all accounts that you have not paid as per agreement, public records you have had, collections, etc. This is your credit's "hurt factory": everything that shows up here is responsible for the bulk of the damage to your credit score.☐

Once you have thoroughly analyzed your credit report, the other thing you need to do is:

Chapter 7: Step 2 – Pinpoint the Credit Score Killers

This chapter picks up from where the previous chapter finished. Once you have gone through your credit reports and especially gone through the negative items sections, you have some idea of the elements that are hurting your credit score.

The next step is to dig deeper and determine which items are truly hurting your credit. Doing this is not hard and is, in fact, something you can easily do yourself. ☐

As previously covered in this book, there are only 5 score factors that determine your credit score. As we have covered as well, these factors do not carry equal weight.

1. Start by examining payment history such as late payments on your report. Again, it is important to know that your payment history will be the most vital factor. 35% of your score will hinge on this. Even a singular late payment will significantly drag down your credit score. If you have several late payments on your report, they are very likely the reason why your credit is doing so badly.

2. The next area to look at is credit utilization, which determines 30% of your credit score. This is inclusive of revolving credit (covered previously in this book, revolving credit points to the likes of credit cards and home equity credit lines). Your credit utilization also

referred to as credit to debt ratio, shows lenders just how responsible you are with your finances. If your credit limit is $10,000 and you owe $9,500 on the credit card, it does not take a genius to figure out why your credit score looks bad.

3. Credit account age plays a serious role in credit score generation, which is why it is bizarre that so many people frequently ditch old credit cards in favor of new ones. An older set of credit cards is an asset, going by age alone, and your credit score will be higher because of it. 15% of your credit score will hinge on this. If your youthful credit account age is the major reason your credit score is poor, the only repair measure is to sit on your lily pad and wait for them to age some more.

4. Do you have a healthy mix of credit accounts? Having a varied mix of accounts, or lack of one, will play a part in determining how high your score is. There are two main credit types: revolving accounts (think in the lines of credit and credit cards) and installment accounts (think student loans, mortgages, car loans, etc.). A creditor likes to see that you can competently handle both credit types.

5. Your credit application history also counts when it comes to your credit score. If you have applied for multiple credit accounts of late, it may explain why your score is less than desirable. 10% of your credit score hinges on this particular subject. This one will take quite some time to fix, but the good news is that the longer you go without accumulating extra credit accounts, the lesser the impact on your score will be.

Once you go through all these factors on your report, you will find out soon enough what is damaging your credit score. What do you do next? One of the fastest ways to see true credit improvement is to fix any errors appearing on your credit report, which is what the next chapter covers.

Chapter 8: Step 3 – Clean Up the Credit Reports

The way to go about cleaning up errors on your credit report is by disputing these errors. You will want to begin your dispute process as soon as you can if you want to see quick improvement on your credit.

Speaking of disputes, you can go about repairing credit on your own, which is actionable enough, or you can use the services of a credit repair professional, which will certainly cost you money but end up worth it in the end. Whatever you choose to do, it is vital that you begin disputing immediately.

Here is a link to a detailed guide showing how to carry out a dispute process:

https://www.credit.com/credit-repair/credit-repair-content/dispute-credit-report-error/

This book will focus on spotting errors and acting with speed to dispute them; however, other than misspellings and outright false information on the credit report, what do you look for when determining what account to dispute? Here are a few red flags:

1. The information is inaccurate. It could be that descriptive details are laid out all wrong, the amounts owed are wrong, or a late payment is still recorded as outstanding even though you have already paid it.

2. The information is untimely. Look out for dates inaccurately recorded. Dates fed all wrong may not mean much to you, but they may definitely mean a lot to a creditor down the line. Besides, why should you accept inaccurately recorded information on something as vital as your credit report?

3. The information is biased. This one is often rare thanks to the staccato, professional nature of credit reports. Nevertheless, do not rule it out altogether.

4. The information is incomplete. It could be that some information is in the record without including the whole package in so that ultimately, it reflects badly on you and by extension, your credit score.

5. The information is questionable. Do you believe that there is information that you can question? Do you feel that some of the things recorded do not reflect your financial activities accurately? Identity theft is a thing that you should be on the lookout for.

NOTE: It is your right as well as the responsibility for an error-free credit report. The nice person act has to make way for necessary action no matter how much you feel like you are being a nuisance to the folks at the bureau. You are obligated to an accurate credit report. Be aggressive and thorough in your attempts to clean up your credit report.

How Difficult Is The Dispute Process?

The answer is simple: it is not. Many people do not realize that while they sit passively, believing the dispute procedure to be too much work, there are thousands of U.S. citizens successfully disputing dubious information on their credit reports every day.

Still, even 10,000 people disputing errors in their credit reports are only a small percentage of Americans. Too many people sabotage their financial health by refusing to dispute unfair errors.

How do you dispute?

Here is a simplistic guide to carrying out a successful dispute:

1. Mail a certified letter to the credit bureau. There is a link in this chapter to a dispute letter guide. Make sure you clearly outline the negative item(s).

2. Make sure you keep a copy of the letter. The credit bureau will undoubtedly get back to you within the month but in case they do not, you could always sue them, and use your letter copy as evidence of their negligence.

3. Disputing your errors online is a bit of a waste of time. There are those who swear by it but it is an open secret that you will get better and quicker results when you bother to write and mail a dispute letter.

4. Detail all the incorrect information in the letter. If you have documents that support your claim, attach copies.

5. Include, clearly and correctly so, all your basic personal information such as your name and address.

6. Use a professional tone all through. It is vital that the bureau takes you seriously. Ranting will only make you seem like a bit of a joke.

7. Once you dispute, the law requires prompt investigation. The law compels the creditor to produce proof of his claim's accuracy.

8. Remember, you may have to go back and forth a few times with the credit bureaus. However, if you keep at it, they will eventually crack.

Once you dispute an error, the credit-reporting agency or bureau has to respond to your claim in the space of one month (30 days) as obligated by law. Thus, you do not have to fear to have to wait indefinitely, and your credit doing badly all along. ☐

Here are additional tips that will help you as you seek to dispute errors in your credit report(s). You may have to write more than one letter as you attempt to have errors cleared from your report:

1. Dispute each mistake with each bureau. Some people believe that disputing a mistake that recurs on all 3 credit reports with one bureau will fix everything. If you do this, the likeliest result is that one credit report will come up clean while the others will still carry the errors.

2. It is common to find more than one error in a credit report. Attempting to dispute all the errors that appear in a wholesale fashion where you lump everything in one dispute letter and send it to the bureaus is a good way to send a message that your dispute does not need seriousness. It is paramount that you dispute each account separately.

3. There is an exception to the above point. If you see several mistakes on one account, it is all right to group the entire pile of mistakes into a single dispute.

4. It is very possible to dispute errors without necessarily using the services of an expert and indeed, many people have done it and achieved success. However, it may be confusing, especially when errors appear sporadically in different credit reports. A reputable credit repair corporation or a lawyer will charge you a fee, but you can guarantee that the job will be thorough.

5. Speaking of credit repair companies, the company that promises you an outright 300-point leap in your score is selling you a pile of nonsense. In fact, even if this was somehow possible, the truth is that it would be almost impossible to accomplish without illegal, Black Hand tactics.

Here is a [link](#) showing what a sample repair letter looks like:

https://www.credit.com/credit-repair/credit-repair-letters/

After this, the next step is to:

Chapter 9: Step 4 – Evaluate Accounts in Collections & Continue Closely Monitoring Your Credit

These are two distinct aspects of repairing your credit scores and therefore, we will look at them individually:

How to Evaluate Accounts in Collections

Take a closer look at your recent collections. Payment history has the biggest impact on your credit score—at least looking at the 35% influence accompanying it. However, the credit score of most Americans suffers mostly because of the state of their collections.

Recent collections inflict the most damage to the average American's credit score seeing as the penalization of newer debt is significantly heavier when coming up with a credit score. It is also important to pay attention to the debt type you are carrying and paying off.

Here are a few gems of debt and paying it off:

1. Medical debts tend not to affect your credit score with the same viciousness as other debt kinds do. Thus, do not make medical debt your first object of focus.

2. When making a debt payment, if you can, make full payments. There is no crime in making partial payments, but partial payments may only reset the time limit, with regard to how long the accounts remain in your report, which may have a bad influence on your score for a longer time.

3. Too many people refuse to consider settlements as a way of getting financially freer and fixing their credit. Attempt to negotiate a settlement with the collection agency. A negotiation settlement will see you pay less than the amounts you owe. If there ever was a downside to doing this, it is that you may have to report the exact amount dismissed as income. Doing this on your tax return information could well result in heavier taxes. You could even go up a higher income bracket, meaning you will be subject to a higher tax rate.

4. On occasion, a collection agency will pretend to be blind to your efforts to pay off debt and will go on acting as though you have made no effort to pay off debt. To avoid such frauds, make sure all payment agreements are in writing and that you have copies. It will be very hard for the collection agency to dismiss your claims in court when you have written documents.

Continue Monitoring your Credit Score

You have taken care of accounts in collections. Make sure that the changes you have made find their way onto your credit report. It is certainly too ambitious to expect the changes to appear next week, but within a couple of months, maximum, the accounts should have dropped off.

Wait at least 8 weeks, check your credit report again, and raise the issue with the credit bureau if you find nothing has changed. How do you do this? You follow the information in the previous chapter on disputing your credit report.

The next step now is to take a proactive approach to repairing your credit score. The next chapter/step talks about how to so this

Chapter 10: Step 5 – Start a Positive Credit History

Beyond disputing errors and staying away from irresponsible financial behavior that reflects badly on your credit score, one of the most potent ways to fix your credit is to go on and start to build a positive credit history.

We call it positive history because the actions you take today will indeed be history a few months or years from now. It could be that a lender has denied you credit today, but this does not mean complete borrowing prohibition.

This brings us to this vital point with regard to building a positive credit history. If your credit utilization, payment history, or account mix are all keeping you away from a good credit score, it is a good strategy to open new credit, which may help you build up your credit at a faster rate. Enter the secured credit card...

The Secured Credit Card

We will describe the secured credit card as "a card meant to help you" and indeed, secured credit cards are powerful tools when it comes to building your credit.

The secured card requires you to pitch in a deposit amount. This deposit amount will double up and serve as your credit limit. If you are late in paying your bills, the card company may dip into your deposit for the amounts owed.

Still, the point of opening this kind of card, as well as doing all other activities to improve your credit, is to combine them with responsible financial behavior: pay your bills on time and make sure your credit utilization speaks well of you. A person with a $1,000 deposit, which means a $1,000 credit limit on the secured card, is making no headway at all if he/she goes ahead and charges $800 from said card.

BENEFITS OF A SECURED CREDIT CARD

Depending on where you are, with regard to your financial and credit state, a secured card could see you make significant credit headway in as little as 6 months. Well, you could see changes within a month, but the key word here is "significant." Here are some benefits that come with a secured card:

1. The secured credit card presents a way to obtain higher credit scores even when unpleasant negative items remain in your report. You may be unapproved for a traditional credit card but most of the time, still be eligible for a secured credit card as they present less risk for the creditor.

2. Moreover, your card issuer will make a point of reporting to the bureaus that you are a fellow with the ability to pay the card on time, which will reflect well on your score.

3. If you were to default on your payment, the security deposit on your card will be the one used. Using the security deposit will mean that even though you default, the card will still be paid, seeing as your funds "secure

it." This phenomenon is why we refer to it as a secured credit card.

With the 5 steps we have discussed in the last few chapters, your credit repair journey should be well on its way, full steam ahead. The next chapter has some essential tips and a few fast tried & tested tips that will boost your credit in a short time span

Section 4: Tried & Tested Tips That Will Boost Your Credit Score Fast

Chapter 11: Quick Strategies You Can Implement To Give Your Credit a New Look in a Short Time

Having negative items struck out of your credit report may see your credit score improve rapidly. However, having a negative item removed will usually take a lot of time. Still, even as you follow the directives of this chapter, it is important that you do your best to have negative items removed. Having said that, let us move on...

Suppose you are looking for quick developments, with regard to your credit score getting healthier. Suppose you only have a couple of months to bump up your credit score. This chapter will show you several fixes that will greatly influence your credit score in a short space of time:

Fix #1: Lower the Credit Utilization Ratio

This book has more than adequately covered credit utilization. The closer you are to maxing out your cards, the more unfortunate the state of your credit will be and the lower the credit score shall be.

How do you lower your credit utilization ratio? You do it by paying down credit card balances. Begin with maxed out cards, or close to it, as this is where the real rot is. Clearing out several maxed out cards could see you attain a 100-point score jump, which is not a small thing.

Fix #2: Request an Increase in Your Credit Card Limits

What happens if you are in no position to pay off multiple debts on your multiple credit cards? There is still a chance of making score improvements. The thing to do is to pick up your phone and request one, or several of your credit card companies, to increase your credit card limit.

It is not in your interest to charge a higher amount than you owe already. All you want is to have a higher credit card limit. In case you have not drawn a conclusion yet, a higher credit limit will mean that the balance you owe takes up a smaller percentage of available credit. In other words, the result is a better credit utilization ratio.

Here is an example.

Assume you owe $5,000 on a credit card that has a $10,000 limit. As it stands, your credit utilization is at 50%, which is not too impressive to the lender, and the algorithm that spits out your credit score. However, if you can have your credit limit bumped up to $15,000; your credit utilization will immediately drop to 35%, assuming you do not go ahead and charge more on the same card.

It will help to have a positive payment history when you make the call. The card company will be more inclined to hear you out if you have a record of making payments on time.

HOW TO REPAIR YOUR CREDIT ALL BY YOURSELF

Fix #3: Become an Authorized User

It is a shame that more people do not use this tactic despite its immense effectiveness and requires almost total passiveness from your part. To implement it, find a close relative or friend. Make sure that this character has a strong, long-standing credit and proceed to ask him or her if you can become an authorized user on an account or two that they own. The account will promptly become part of your report… in its entirety. If the person's credit is truly strong, you could see as much as a 100-point score increase in a matter of weeks, all from doing little more than ask.

Of course, there are more than a few risks involved with this one. Your friend could decide to go over to the dark side and refuse to make payments, or consistently start making late payments. Your friend could also be carrying a large balance on his account. The goodwill appears hand in hand with the bad, and you can expect to see it all laid out on your credit report. The tactic, simply put, requires caution.

Fix #4: Consolidate Credit Card Debt

Another potent way to repair your credit score fast is to consider a debt consolidation loan. This one is somewhat like fighting fire with fire, but it actually works. This sort of loan is a personal loan type that you will channel toward paying off the various credit cards in your possession. You then pay a singular monthly balance on this personal loan.

You may be able to save some good money by getting a lower interest rate on the loan (this will require that you negotiate with the lender), but this will be dependent on the interest rates on your credit cards. If they are not too high, then you stand a good chance.

Still, even if the credit card interest rates are through the roof, it is possible to find a lender who will still slash off the loan rate anyway. Arm yourself with a preapproval and shop around for the best rates. As far as the monthly payments on this sort of loan go, you could break even, and your credit score would still see a marked increase. This is because this loan falls into the installment loan category, a category viewed more favorably.

Fix #5: Consider Getting a Credit Building Loan

You will have to approach smaller banks, or banks steeped away from the traditional bank format. Smaller banks, even credit unions, offer credit builder loans to individuals who want to fix their credit issues.

Once you take out the loan, the lender will deposit the money into a secured account. So secured is this account that in fact, you will not be able to access it. You will then proceed with making payments toward the loan on a monthly basis. Only when you repay the entire loan will the lender releases the funds so you can use them. It is a lot like unlocking levels on a video game.

Making payments on monies you cannot spend seems a bit bizarre. Still, it makes sense: the bank has to protect itself, and this move offers you a proper chance to prove that you can be a responsible adult as far as the issue of borrowed money goes.

HOW TO REPAIR YOUR CREDIT ALL BY YOURSELF

Even better, once you complete making the payments, the bank will go ahead and report to the credit bureaus that you are a borrower who is able to pay his dues on time. This will have a positive effect on your credit score.

Section 5: What to Expect (and What Next) After Fixing Your Credit Score

Chapter 12: How Long It Takes To Overhaul Your Credit Score

With the right strategies—such as those contained in the previous chapter—and an aggressive, determined mindset, you could go a long way toward improving your score in 30 days. You could even be able to improve your score by 100+ points, which is quite phenomenal.

It is true that you can make significant headway in a month. However, how long will it take to really turn your credit around and have it at an excellent state? How long will it take you to fix your credit completely so that the unpleasant items disappear completely? From a realistic standpoint, how long will a complete overhaul take?

The answer to the questions is certainly not 30 days. Even a couple of years would be ambitious unless you either had very few negative items in place or somehow successfully applied to have every negative item on your credit report removed.

Credit revisions usually take time. Some people think that if you dispute everything on your credit report, you will somehow compel the bureaus to revise your credit. However, it is pointless to dispute accurate information on your report. If you indeed made 3 late payments in the last financial year and your creditor reported this, all a dispute will do is waste your time, the bureau's time, and that of the creditor—and the negative item will still reappear next time.

THE 7 YEAR LIMIT

Typically, most negative items take 7 years to age off and fall off your report with the exceptions being bankruptcies and unpaid tax liens that often hang around for at least a decade.

With this said, you do not have to sit passively and wait for the negative items to fall off. One great strategy to have the negative items removed, especially if you have since paid off the outstanding amounts, is to write to your creditor and request to have the item removed. It is true that a mere request may get you your desired revision (they call it goodwill), but it is likelier that you will have to settle for some financial settlement or other, in order for them to remove the negative item. Nevertheless, expect the process to take some time, since your creditor may insist on checking your recent financial record to determine if you deserve having the item taken off your report.

STEADY IMPROVEMENTS SHOULD CONTRIBUTE TO THE BIGGER PICTURE

With all of this said, while you may have to wait several years to see a total overhaul of your credit situation, you could see significant, marked improvements every few weeks, especially if you combine the credit repair strategies covered in the previous chapter with responsible credit handling.

Here is a strategy that will help keep your credit score improvement consistent. Since the typical American is obsessed with his or her credit card, ensure you keep your credit utilization at 30% or below. Let us now look at how to ensure that your credit health remains great.

Chapter 13: What To Do To Keep Your Credit Health Excellent

It is well and good to take care of negative items in your report that are dragging down your credit score. However, what is the point of doing this and then picking up fresh negative items?

Credit repair will take unnecessarily long to implement successfully if you do not overhaul your financial activity. Here are tips that will help you maintain the credit score increases that you worked so hard to achieve.

Tip #1: Draw up A Budget and Stick to It

If there ever were a rule on keeping the credit on track and generally improving finance, it would read like this: ***Live within your means.***

It may not always be the case, but in some case, you will find the need to take on a loan because some emergency or other came up. This is why, no matter how effective you are at making your paycheck stretch out over a month, you should save some money every month so that you do not have to take out credit so frequently, damaging your credit in the process.

Be responsible with your credit card. If you are a typical American with a penchant for whipping out the credit card, it is very likely that your card is the major reason behind your poor credit. Avoid making unnecessary purchases with frequency because you get closer to having your card maxed out this way.

Check your account every evening before you go to bed so you have an idea how your finances are faring. By and by, and with responsible behavior, you will get closer to an excellent credit score.

Tip #2: Pay All Your Bills on Time

By now, you know that a large portion of your credit score—35% to be specific—hinges on your payment history. Payment history is not truly emphatic on whether you actually made your payments so much as it is on how timely your payments were. Even one late payment can seriously hurt your credit.

Ensure you know how much you owe in bills each month, and make sure you pay every bill. Even better, why not have an automated system agreed with your bank that will see allowed amounts automatically channeled toward paying off respective bills?☐

Tip #3: Get Your Secured Credit Card and Use It Responsibly

We have already covered the secured credit card and all the benefits that come with one. Be responsible for this card. Remember that the deposit amount you put in also acts as your credit limit. Keep the debt to credit ratio at 30% or below. Otherwise, keep working on increasing the card's credit limit if you figure that you will need to take out larger amounts in the future.

ERNIE BRAVEBOY

BONUS SECTION: MORTGAGE APPLICATION AND POOR CREDIT SCORE

Bonus: A Mini-Guide on Mortgage Application for Those with Poor Credit

You may be tired of parting with rental fees every month or it could be that you have decided that it is about time you bought a house and start building equity. Unfortunately, it is difficult to be an attractive prospect for home loans if your credit is bad. In fact, only people who have a minimum score of 750 are ideal home loan candidates—these fellows get the most competitive interest rates.

As such, if your credit repair strategy implementation has not gotten you out of your credit bog, you may have to deal with more than a few mortgage denials or absurdly high-interest rates on the mortgages you can find. Still, this does not mean that it is impossible to get a mortgage and a competitive one at that.

First, let us examine the challenges that come with purchasing a house on poor credit.

Challenges of Buying Your Home When Your Credit Score is Poor

If your credit score is lower than 750, which it most likely is, you may have to accept that the most competitive mortgage rates in the market are off the table for you. Try to see things from the lender's point of view: the fellow with the higher credit score obviously poses a lower risk—with regard to a foreclosure in the future—or defaulting on the loan.

It thus makes sense to make the most competitive rates exclusive to them. If your score is poor, the Mortgage Company views you as a risky loan prospect. You may have to pay higher interest rates if you do manage to get a mortgage.

WHAT ARE YOUR OPTIONS?

The first step is to find out where your credit stands. Is your credit merely average without being spectacular or is it outright awful?

If even after applying quick credit repair strategies, your score still cannot crack 650, then it is about time you start researching on the "home loans with poor credit" topic. There is some good news for you though. These days, there are multiple programs available for first-time homebuyers (think the likes of Federal Housing Administration (FHA) loans) or people who want to buy a home with underwhelming credit.

FHA loans are a godsend, especially seeing as a score of 580 will still see you eligible for a home loan, provided you can put up a 3.5% down payment on the home. You also do not have to have 2 years of employment under your belt to qualify for FHA loans, a stipulation that comes with most loans.

Consider the HOPE program as well. The program allows people with poor credit to be approved for a home loan with a 0% down payment outlay. It is a neat program; you will be able to build your credit as you make payments going forward.

Besides both FHA and HOPE programs, you can consider saving up for a bigger down payment (or opting for a smaller, cheaper home). When you can put up a bigger down payment, you will be able to borrow less, which may raise the chances of being eligible for a mortgage.

Conclusion

We have come to the end of the book. Thank you for reading and congratulations on reading until the end.

As this book so clearly outlines, you are not doomed to lugging around your poor credit. With astute measures and responsible financial behavior, you will be able to inject new life into your credit.

The idea is to combine responsible financial behavior with the implementation of credit repair strategies. If you are consistent with this combined approach, you will begin to see marked improvements in a short time.

It is also important to point out that credit repair is not as hectic as some people make it out to be. While professional services tend to bring a refined, progressive approach to credit repair, fixing your credit is something you can succeed at on your own, as this book has so clearly shown.

If you found the book valuable, can you recommend it to others? One way to do that is to post a review on Amazon.

Please leave a review for this book on Amazon!

Thank you and good luck!

Get Your Free Copy of

How to be a Real Estate Millionaire

To Get Your Free Copy, Open the Link

https://ebraveboy_3ee2.gr8.com/

www.ingramcontent.com/pod-product-compliance
Lightning Source LLC
Chambersburg PA
CBHW052316220526
45472CB00001B/137